ALSO BY DR. CURTIS E. SMITH

"When It's Time," - An Inspirational Work

"See, Point, and Say, Communication Guide"- A
Self-help Guide for Handicapped

"A Hospice Guide Book," – An Educational Work;
Everything you need to know about Hospice

"Walking Through The Valley,"- An Inspirational Work

And Soon to be Published

"A Positive Thought A Day, Keeps the Negative Away" – 365
Inspirational Thoughts For the Day With Supporting Scripture Verses

The
APPLIED
POWER *of*
POSITIVE
THINKING

DR. CURTIS E. SMITH, PHD, PSYD

Inspiring Voices®
A Service of Guideposts

Scripture taken from the King James Version of the Bible.

Cover Illustration by Steve Dunn - A Professional Graphic Design Artist, Irvine, CA

Inspiring Voices books may be ordered through booksellers or by contacting:

Inspiring Voices
1663 Liberty Drive
Bloomington, IN 47403
www.inspiringvoices.com
1 (866) 697-5313

ISBN: 978-1-4624-0881-8 (sc)
ISBN: 978-1-4624-0880-1 (e)

Library of Congress Control Number: 2014900209

Printed in the United States of America.

Inspiring Voices rev. date: 01/30/2014

LEGAL DISCLAIMER

The written material presented in this publication *The Applied Power of Positive Thinking* is the exclusive property of the author, with the exception of clichés, idioms and Biblical quotes commonly used in the Public Domain.

It is neither the intent of the author to plaragize, or to intentionally use copyrighted materials without permission of the copyright holder.

In no event shall the author, namely Dr. Curtis E. Smith, be liable for any special, direct, indirect, or consequential damages or any damages whatsoever resulting from information, arising out of, or in connection with, the use or performance of any information appearing in this publication.

In the unlikely event, that any copyrighted material inadvertently appears herewith __ with the exception of newspaper articles used in part and articles appearing in the Public Domain that may be presented __ the author claims hold harmless privilege.

CONTENTS

Part II—RELATIONSHIPS: The Marital Dyad; the Nuclear Family

DEDICATION

The Applied Power of Positive Thinking is dedicated to Dr. Robert H. Schuller, Founder and Ex-Officio Minister of the Crystal Cathedral, Garden Grove California, who endorsed my first book, titled *"When It's Time."* Dr. Schuller is also a protégé of the late Dr. Norman Vincent Peal, both for whom I hold great admiration and respect.

I also dedicate this book to the memory of Dr. Norman Vincent Peale, an Icon in the field of positive thinking who without question, touched and enhanced the lives of millions of people who were positively influenced by his classic work *The Power of Positive Thinking*.

I would be remiss if I did not mention in dedication Dr. James Kok, Director Pastoral Care Department, for the Crystal Cathedral. "Jim," as he is fondly called by colleagues and friends, served as my mentor in the Clinical Pastoral Education Training Program conducted by the Crystal Cathedral. Under his guidance and teaching the ability to "get in touch" with my own personal inner feelings was enhanced.

The work is also dedicated to those who have adopted the essence of Positive and Possibility Thinking to their life, as well as to their vocabulary, and *have*, and *are*, using positive thought to improve and enrich their lives.

Additionally, I dedicate the book to my colleagues and friends, who have assisted me in putting my thoughts into words, and facilitating *The Applied* **Power of Positive** *Thinking*, plus Possibility Thought ____ along with strong faith in God, accompanied by Spirituality ____ in achieving whatever level of success I may have attained.

Finally, I dedicate this work, *The Applied Power of Positive Thinking*, to my faithful and lovely wife Sandra, who is not only beautiful on the *outside*, but passionately sustains a profound compassion, emotion and love on the *inside* for those with whom she comes into contact.

ACKNOWLEDGMENT

For unlimited help received from those who have made suggestions for subject inclusion, and the learned insight offered by those who read the manuscript, and have offered helpful tips for better presentation of material discussed, I am deeply touched and extremely grateful.

FRONT COVER: I am very appreciative of Steve Dunn, the Graphic Design Artist, Irvine, CA, who designed and produced the art work for the front cover.

The design appropriately captures the theme of *The Applied Power of Positive Thinking by* depicting female and male images *absorbed* in thought and by using the globe illustration implies the embracement of generic audiences from around the world.

At the risk and embarrassment of leaving out someone, I will not attempt to name each of those who have made valuable contributions for enhancement and improvement to this work. Each of you knows who you are that has given invaluable insights and suggestions.

Rest assured; I am very grateful.

To each one, thank you, and God bless *you* as you pursue *your Applied Power of Positive Thinking.*

PREFACE

Throughout the history of civilization humankind has experienced problems. Problems for which there are few, if any, totally satisfactory, workable, individual or collective solutions.

Subsequently, men and women have turned to psychiatrists, psychologists, marriage and family therapists, pastors, priests, rabbis and other clergy persons for help in arriving at *"an answer;"* at the same time, recognizing there is no *"one size fits all solution,"* that can be equally, and successfully, applied to *"all"* circumstances, issues, problems, and situations.

It is with that thought in mind, that this work is presented. As a psychotherapist, pastoral counselor, marriage-family therapist, and pastor for more than thirty years, it is the intent of the author to provide common-sense, doable, workable and proved, alternative solutions for many problems ____ which should be thought of as "issues"____ that can be credibly and viably applied, not as "Band-Aid solutions," rather, as lasting, long-term solutions for ordinary common problems and issues.

The author is not naive to the point of believing, that there are *"right"* or *"wrong"* answers to every circumstance or situation; to the contrary, there are many shades of gray.

Obviously, what works well for one person, does not ____ or will not ____ always work for another. There are two sides to every circumstance or situation. Recognizing this fact, that there is not always a right or wrong answer or solution, the question then should be: Are the solutions presented in this book practical, doable, and more importantly, do the dynamics of *the power of applied positive thinking* presented, "fit" the circumstance or situation facilitate a workable, long-lasting solution?

That is the question the readers___ whether male or female, young or old ___must necessarily ask, in order to obtain the maximum individual, or group benefit from this work; connecting the application, via *the power of applied positive t*hinking, and possibility thought, *for* actual, and realistic *positive* living.

In 1952 Norman Vincent Peale wrote a book called *The Power of Positive Thinking.* Some say *"next to the Bible, it is the greatest inspirational book of our time."*

Others say, *"Millions have found fearless confidence, a life of radiant faith and vitality in t*he reading of *The Power of Positive Thinking."*

Many believe that Dr. Peale's book has been instrumental in proving that, *"an attitude of the mind can change lives and win success in all things, and overcome all obstacles."* It is also believed that his book teaches if you have a problem, there is a solution. If you are in despair, or feeling helpless, there is help, and if there is hopelessness, there is hope for happiness and renewed confidence in life. There is no denying any of these dynamics.

The premise of this work, ***The Applied Power of Positive Thinking,*** is to transform obstacles into opportunities by pointing out the "HOW TO" Formula *to achieve* successful living through positive thinking by *combining* three dynamics; that is, a *positive mental attitude (*PMA), *plus* the power of *positive thinking* plus *possibility thought,* and *achieve* desired end results by facilitating ***The Applied Power of Positive Thinking.***

SYNOPSIS

In 1955, Dr. Robert H. Schuller, strongly influenced by Dr. Peale ____ of whom it could be said Dr. Peale was his Mentor ____ founded the first drive-in church; the Garden Grove Community Church ____ at the Orange Drive-in Theater, Orange, California (In 1980 the church was re-named the Crystal Cathedral). Dr. Schuller focused his attention and teaching on the positive aspects of Christianity and emphasized *uplifting* theology and *possibility thinking.*

As important and beneficial as the teachings of these religious icons is, for millions of people, it appears that *both only scratched the surface* by presenting formulas, opinions, philosophies, and theories *for* positive thought, and possibility thinking, and have *overlooked* the *"how to" method* and *means for credible and viable application* to *bring about* positive change.

Thus, in the philosophy of both, there appears to be an *omission* in setting forth a *practical way* to *apply* the teachings of *the power of positive thinking* and *possibility thought,* to enable a favorable end result *for* successful living.

Subsequently, it is the intent of this work, *The Applied Power of Positive Thinking* to explain from a practical, therapeutic perspective point-of-view, "HOW **TO**" bring a positive mental attitude ____ PMA as the author likes to think of it ____ into focus, and successfully facilitate to fruition *The Applied Power of Positive Thinking.*

By *combining* three dynamics, that is, a *positive mental attitude* (PMA), *plus* the *applied power of positive thinking*, plus *possibility thought,* and *applying* the "HOW TO" Formula *to achieve* successful living through positive thinking.

Subsequently, presenting a *contrast* and *comparison* between **Opinion, Philosophy** and **Theory vs.** *a practical, therapeutic perspective point-of-view.*

These combined dynamics, the *Application* of (DMA), **Desire, Motivation,** *and* **Application,** plus positive thought, form the foundation for *The Applied Power of Positive Thinking.*

PART I

INDIVIDUALS:
Personal Perspectives

CHAPTER 1

You Are Not Alone

When a person is faced with, a difficult circumstance or situation which they do not know how to deal with to a successful conclusion, they invariably believe the circumstance or situation is *unique* to them alone. Nothing could be farther from the truth.

Somewhere in the world, at any given time, literally thousands of other individuals are experiencing same or similar circumstances or situations. *You are not alone.*

The Holy Scriptures says, *"...there is nothing new under the sun."* Ecclesiastes 1:9.KJV. With this thought in mind, realistically a conclusion can be reached; life situations *are* repetitious.

A thirty-five year practice as a Psychotherapist, Pastoral Counselor, Marriage / Family Therapist, and Minister, thousands of stories have come to the fore-front, in both individual and con-joint therapy, with persons whom I have counseled. Everyone has a story, and while the faces, places, personalities have changed, many of the stories are same or similar with regard to affairs, anger, parenting, alcohol and drug abuse, blame, mental abuse, physical abuse, sexual abuse, employment abuse, marriage dynamics, and on, and on.

Perhaps the loneliest time an individual experiences, when going through depression, trials, tribulation, problems and issues is the thought that *'I am the only one in the world who feels like this.'* As previously indicated __ though this may seem a reality ____ it is simply

1

not true. At this very moment, while you are reading this, there are literally tens of thousands of persons who have mixed emotional features about whatever issue they may be facing. At the same time a majority of them believe __ or at least think __ that they are the *only* person in the world facing circumstances, problems and situations.

In this work, **The Applied Power of Positive Thinking**, examination and discussion will be made over each area listed in the index; a comparison will be made and contrasted with real life cases, from which the author has conducted therapy, that will be presented where doable, realistic, and workable solutions have been successfully accomplished.

Without breaching confidentiality, or violating any individual privacy, or HIPPA regulations, it is the intent of this critique to bring to the fore-front, focus on, and offer doable, workable, viable and long-lasting alternative solutions to those who may be experiencing difficulties and issues and are seeking doable, workable, proven solutions for what may seem to be impossible circumstances.

Solution which comes through facilitation of *the applied power of positive thinking* and the subtle influence of possibility thought.

Solution examples will be presented in a brief literary sketch synopsis format, commonly known in counseling therapy as Vignettes.

A Vignette, based on an actual experience, is presented, which can be considered to be a hypothesis.

The readers need to keep in mind that, there are no *"easy, quick-fix"* solutions, nor is there a *"one-size-fits-all"* solution that will *"fit all"* circumstances, difficulties, or situations.

Rather, "working through" circumstances, difficulties and seemingly impossible situations is hard, and sometimes difficult work.

After choosing an alternative answer, or tentative doable and workable solution path, the hard work commences with the application of positive thought, coupled with desire, and strong motivation.

Although you __ the reader __ may think you are the *only person* in the world facing a particular experience you are faced with and going through, just know; *you are not alone.*

Vignette:

John and Carla were newlyweds. Married for less than a year Carla was pregnant. They were very excited about the pregnancy and looked forward to being parents. A dark secret emerged from the closet; John had neglected to tell Carla that he was a recovering drug addict.

He later tried to justify concealing the truth by saying that he *"had seen no need to bring up the subject since I (he) had been clean and sober for over two years."*

The inevitable happened; John had a relapse and did not come home one night. Carla was worried sick. She called John's mother who bared the ugly truth; John had a history of re-lapsing, going into denial, finally going cold-turkey, getting clean and sober, and then re-lapsing again. Since the mother believed John to be an honest person she was very surprised that he had not told Carla about his addiction recovery.

Carl's mother helped Carla to locate him, helped to get him sober, and brought him back home to be with Carla. He pleaded deep remorse and sorrow for his actions, said "it won't happen again," and seemed to straighten up for a time. He had managed to start his own electrical business, had secured a number of commercial accounts, and was earning a good salary as an electrician business owner/operator.

In a relatively short time John's confident promise to Carla that "it won't happen again," became an empty promise. John re-lapsed. This time he called Carla from a motel room he had rented and told her that he was not coming home until he used up all of the coke he had bought from a dealer."

To make a long story shorter, this pattern continued. John ultimately "snorted up" all of the money they had saved from his business, and soon did not have enough money to even pay his operating expenses and for materials he had purchased to run the electrical business. One by one he lost the accounts he had established to other electrical contractors. For both Carla and John the situation went from bad, to worse, to terrible. Carla, a devout Christian, began to pray and think positively about the circumstances.

Others she talked with, including family members, tried to persuade her to leave and divorce John. She refused, and took solace in believing that if she were patient and kept a positive attitude that John would come to his senses and that they could re-establish their marriage and enjoy a family.

In the meantime, Carla moved in with her divorcee mother, went full term with the pregnancy, and gave birth to a healthy, baby boy. She continued to positively believe in her heart of hearts that John was going to recover, straighten up and resume his role as husband and father.

She eventually lost contact with John who was now homeless and living on the street. From time to time she would hear from John's mother, brother, or father. She last heard that he had robbed a grocery store for money to buy drugs, and that he was now in jail. She kept on expressing a positive mental attitude, praying and believing that eventually all would be well.

She then learned that John had been released from jail, but that he had been picked-up again for a DUI; driving under the influence of a controlled substance. Beyond reasonable belief she never gave up hope and diligently applied and maintained positive thinking.

Several years passed wherein she was forced to start receiving social service assistance through the median of Aid for Dependent Children; during his incarceration she had visited him for a conjugal visit in jail, gotten pregnant again, and they now had two children. Despite dire and sometimes desperate circumstances Carla never despaired, lost her hope, or positive belief that one day circumstances would change for the better.

Five years passed her by in her role as a single parent. Then one day, out of the blue, she received a telephone call from John. He told her that he had gone through and "intervention session," had been admitted to re-habilitation, and was, at last, on the road to recovery. He wanted to re-connect with her, and promised that "now things were going to be different."

Carla's heart leaped with joy; her positive mental attitude had finally paid off. She said a silent prayer in reflection and thanksgiving.

Carla and John did re-unite. Clean and sober he pursued his electrician career and landed a job with a major electrical company as an intern.

This time he really was serious, and with strong determination, influenced by wife Carla's positive outlook on life, he has succeeded in staying clean and sober for four years.

John and Carla were able to follow their dream and buy a starter home. They connected with a local church, re-newed their vows of faith in a Higher Power, and began re-building their lives.

Years passed, and they now have five children, one of which has graduated high school and another that will be graduating in two years.

This vignette clearly illustrates what *can happen* in the human life when coupled with faith, prayer and determination, the *applied power of positive thinking* is facilitated.

In summary, a former statement is reiterated: there are many shades of gray and what may appear to be an impossible situation ___ seemingly being experienced only by you ___ just know, *you are not alone.*

A doable, workable solution is always possible by facilitating **the applied power of positive thinking.**

CHAPTER 2

Who Am I? *Who* Do
I Want to Be?

The United States Army has a slogan: *"Be all you can be."*

That statement begs the question: *Who am I? And, who do I want to be?* The answer should be, *"I want to be the best person I know how to be."* This is almost a foregone conclusion, but not always.

Permit me to make a statement that may sound trite, but in fact, is sound and actual, factual truth. The statement is: "You can become whatever you want to be." In the truest sense this *is* positive thinking. Let's take it a step further: No one can be you, like you can be you.

Accept yourself, not for who you presently are, but for who you want to be. The Biblical admonition is: *"As a man thinks in his heart, that so he is."* Proverbs 23:7 KJV.

Let's put all this in a frame of reference:

1. What you think is what you say...
2. What you say is what you become...
3. What you become is what you want to be; until you want to change...
4. You are the only one who *can* change you.

The single most important choice used in helping one's self is to *want* help. Thus, *the desire to want help* is the first step in getting help. Subsequently the single most important

Dynamics are: **DAMA**

1. **Desire**: To receive and accept help, one must want help...
2. **Application** of that desire produces...
3. **Motivation**: Motivation produces action, and action precipitates...
4. **Achievement**: Achievement, is better known as success,

All of these dynamics are proceeded by:

1. A positive mental attitude, which produces action...
2. Action produces positive mental assurance, and confidence, to be the best person an individual can be...
3. No one can be you, like you can be you; *this is a repetitious statement,* but oh, so true!
4. End Result: The act of being you becomes genuine and real

Vignette:

A psychologist doctor colleague and friend, had never been seriously ill a day in his life. This all changed the day he could no longer freely urinate. He had been struggling with voiding for awhile, but dismissed it as some sort of infection that would clear up. The situation became worse and he ended up in the ER, and was subsequently admitted to the hospital. He didn't know what was wrong: he hoped for the best, but feared the worst. He didn't have to wait long. His family doctor entered the hospital room. They exchanged greetings. The doctor removed a stethoscope from around his neck and placed it on my friend's chest. Listening intently he moved the stethoscope around the chest area.

"Your heart seems to be O.K., but I have some disappointing news," he said.

"What is it, doc?" my friend asked.

"You have renal failure. We need to consider and discuss dialysis." the doctor replied."

My colleague and friend reflected on what was being said. Lying in the hospital these last few days he wondered what was going on. He had seen doctor after doctor and now a diagnosis was confirmed; he had renal failure. His kidney's had stopped functioning. He remembered receiving massive doses of medication; but he didn't know what it was, or what it was for. Now it was explained. They had tried to "jump start" his kidneys into working again. The attempts had failed.

He heard the doctor saying, *"We are going to put in a Quinton dialysis (sub-Clavian) catheter. This will be used to hook you up to a dialysis machine."*

The doctor went on to explain why: *"The dialysis will take approximately 3 hours, and is designed to remove impurities from the blood, and to remove excess fluid from the body. These are the first major steps toward saving your life. As soon as possible you will go to surgery for permanent placement of a shunt in the arm. The placement location will be decided by the urologist."*

My friend told me his head was reeling with too much information, but he wanted to know what methods and procedures were going to be used in his treatment. The doctor was still talking.

"The Quinton catheter will be used until the shunt heals and is appropriate for use. After which it will be removed. Your dialysis treatment will continue indefinitely, three times a week for approximately 3 to 4 hours per treatment." The doctor stopped talking and then asked.

"Any questions?"

My friend later told me his head was spinning and that he didn't know what to ask.

He finally answered, *"No. Not at this time."*

"O.K. then, the dialysis technician will educate you as to proper diet, activity and life style. I will see you again in my office in 3 weeks. In the meantime, don't let it get you down. I have dialysis patients who have been on dialysis for years. See you in 3 weeks." The doctor ended the conversation and quickly left the room.

The physician offered sound advice. Becoming a dialysis patient is not fatal. You are not becoming an invalid. With proper diet, exercise and medical care the dialysis patient can lead a near normal life-style with very limited restrictions.

One of the most difficult considerations for a person diagnosed with renal failure is, *"Do I want to become a dialysis patient?"* Many patients choose *not to*, however, numerous patients choose *to undergo dialysis*. My friend chose the latter.

Five years have passed since his diagnosis and start of dialysis treatment. Aside from minor set-backs, which were easily medically addressed, and resolved. He now performs his own personal dialysis at home; it occurs while he sleeps. He tells me, with the application of powerful thinking, he made the "right" decision.

This is another crystal clear example of **how** profound the **applied power of positive Thinking** can beneficially influence the outcome of life circumstances.

In summary, at the risk of being repetitious, some pertinent facts are herewith re-stated:

Accept yourself, not for who you presently are, but for who you want to be. Again, the Biblical admonition is: *"As a man thinks in his heart, that so he is."* Proverbs 23:7 KJV.

Let's put all this in a frame of reference:

1. What you think, is what you say…
2. What you say, is what you become…
3. What you become, is what you want to be; until you want to change…
4. ***You are the only one who, realistically, can CHANGE you.***

The single most important choice used in helping one's self is to *want* help. The desire to want help is the first step in getting help. Someone has said, *"A journey of a thousand miles begins with the first step."* Help begins, by first helping yourself.

Thus, begins the journey, in search of answering the questions of: **Who am I? And, who do I want to be?** The answer should be, *"I want to be the best person I know how to be."*

Rest assured, with God's help, you *can* reach any doable goal within reason, you set out to achieve, by facilitation of the ***applied power of positive thinking.***

CHAPTER 3

Communication

Someone has said, *"I can't hear a word you're saying, because of what I see you doing."*

Thus, a perfect illustration of failed, verbal communication overshadowed by "mixed- message" body language.

I. In order to effectively communicate consistently one needs to "think through" the message they are attempting to convey.

Printed communication, i.e. journalism, uses a bold and familiar criterion for presenting clear thought, comprehensive and concise communication. Their formula is expressed:

1. **Who**
2. **What**
3. **When**
4. **Where**
5. **Why**

A. First and foremost, verbal communication should not be *any less* bold, clear, or familiar.

When speaking publically a good rule of thumb for effective communication is: "Speak like you write; write like you speak."

B. Second, speak to the issue. Too many persons are unfamiliar and unsure of their subject matter. Subsequently, the attempted spoken communication becomes circuitous; the speaker talks in circles, touching on many sub-topic thoughts, and fails to zero in and focus on the one intended subject. This pattern is known in the arena of public speaking as, "rabbit chasing."

C. The circuitous pattern, or "rabbit chasing," usually takes place for two, and probably more, reasons:

   1. The communicator / speaker is not familiar with the subject matter and does not *know* what they are talking about, or…
   2. The communicator / speaker is trying to impress the listener with fragmented information hoping to appear learned on the subject

To present direct, effective, verbal communication the speaker should have substantial knowledge about the subject being presented.

The speaker needs to use as few words as possible to express and convey clear, comprehensive, and unburdened thought. An old motto regarding speech is:

"Don't use 10 words, when 5 words will do!"

II. Don't be a *"know-it-all."*

When speaking, aside from knowing the subject well, it is good to speak with a voice of authority. However, don't appear to be a "know-it-all" as some speakers pretend to be.

In addition, when possible, offer participation ____ if not verbally from an audience ____ at least attempt to inspire, *with thoughtful speaking*, involvement of the active listener from a mental perspective.

The active listener remains far more interested in hearing what is being said when they *know* they will have an opportunity to respond, if not during the presentation, at least with the speaker, after the presentation during question and answer time.

The wise and mature speaker uses greater wisdom when the verbalization is peppered with statements such as: it appears," "I think;" "I believe;" "It seems to me;" "It is my opinion," etc. This form of communication is open-ended, and is an un-spoken invitation for the active listener to join the conversation either mentally or verbally.

Informal, face-to-face, two way conversations / are also enhanced when the primary spokesperson offers a spoken participation invitation by asking "What do you think?"

III. Be an active listener

Too often, in two way conversations, the listener is so busy trying to interrupt the speaker ____ to respond before a full statement has been made by the speaker ____ that almost everything that is being said by the speaker, is falling on listener deaf ears, and, is lost to the listener.

One has to learn how to become an "active listener."

Perhaps the reader is wondering, "How does being able to communicate effectively factor into applying the power of positive thinking?" This is a reasonable and valid question.

The answer, in one word, is "respect," whether to another as speaker, or to you as an active listener as you interact with others in society. This is very important.

Without respect to you, from others, and your respect for them, what does it matter whether or not you ever apply the power of positive thinking? You could just as well become a hibernating hermit.

Being able to effectively communicate your mind and thoughts clearly is truly a mark of the applied power of positive thinking.

To summarize: Positive, clear communication, to say what you mean, and to mean what you say, and the learned ability for active listening, is the hallmark for application of *the applied power of positive thinking.* Even the Almighty said*: "Be still and know that I am God."* Psalms 46:10 KJV.

This Biblical admonition could be paraphrased to say: *"Be still, and know that I am... speaking."* Psalms 46:10 KJV.

Communication is an art; the act of effective speaking and active listening, coupled with clear and positive thinking, appropriately sums up effective clear, direct, thought-provoking communication.

Another bold communication statement:

"Stand up, speak up; shut up!"

In other words: when you effectively convey your talking points, emphasize the points, and close the presentation, you have very successfully illustrated *the power of applied positive thinking*

CHAPTER 4

Be YOU; *No One,* Can Be YOU, Like YOU Can Be YOU!

With reference to the individual the title of this chapter literally says it all.

Be you; no one, can be you, like you can be you!

There is a mindset being floated in our society today which flies in the face of intelligent Design, Biblical fact. For instance, with regard to male to female; female to male. Some believe that, when they were born (created) the genetic design formulation was flawed by a genetic mutation. Therefore, in their mind they were born male, but were in fact, supposed to be female. or vice versa. Subsequently, there is a perpetual struggle, the belief of being *unnaturally* born as the *"wrong gender."*

Medical science has played into the hands of this minority by alluding to, and in fact, performing surgery to "correct" the so-called error of nature. Subsequently, from a medical perspective, medical science has the capability to "correct the error," (their term), caused by nature, through surgically transforming a male into a female, or conversely, transforming a female into a male. This process is known as "genetic engineering."

And while medical technology can, through genetic engineering, surgically, and physically change the external anatomy of an individual, the fact remains that through the natural process of birthing they are still whatever gender they were created as, and born with: male or female.

Again, if one subscribes to Intelligent Design, we again cite the Intelligent Design dynamic spoken of in the creation story as recorded in the Old Testament book of Genesis: *"God created…male and female…"* Genesis 1:27 KJV. *From the New Testament, "Have you not read that he who made them from the beginning made them male and female?"* Matthew 19:4.

Someone has said: *"Looks are deceiving,"* and *"all that glitters, is not gold."* And so it would appear to be with mankind. A man is a man, is a man; a woman is a woman, is a woman.

Especially for persons who accepts and believes in Intelligent Design. Because for them, in their belief system, this seeming "medical miracle" procedure flies in the face of creation by the intelligent designer; namely, God.

When an individual accepts and believes in Intelligent Design, they usually also believe the Bible to be literal Biblical history, and therefore, accept as biblical fact the Biblical account of creation recorded in the book of Genesis, to be historically accurate.

The creation account in Genesis, Chapter 1, verse 26, has God saying; *"…let us make man in our image, after our likeness."* KJV

And again, in Genesis, Chapter 1, verse 27, *"So God created man in his own image, in the image of God created he him; male and female created he them."* KJV

For those who subscribe to Biblical teaching, that is, Christians and Protestants, they would confess: *"God said it, I believe it, and that settles it."*

However, for those who neither believe in, or subscribe to, Intelligent Design or an Intelligent Designer, i.e. a Higher Power, their statement presumably would be: *"I don't believe it (the Bible) therefore, I cannot receive it,"* that is, the Biblical account of creation by an Intelligent Designer as recorded in the Old Testament Book of Genesis.

These persons usually subscribe to the position of Atheist, i.e. "*There is no God,*" and fall into the category of an anti-God, non-believer mindset, or an evolutionary, 'survival of the fittest,' Darwin evolution theory. That is, that man evolved from an ape or gorilla theory.

On the other hand, there is a mindset of Agnosticism, which says that "*maybe there is a God, but if so, he has no interest in what is happening here on planet earth, and he certainly does not have an interest in, nor does he care, what happens to humankind; no further interest in his creation*" (if he is the creator).

This mind set leaves open the possibility there is a higher power; at least, they acknowledge the possibility that he does exist.

All of these mind sets and theories fly in the face of positive thinking. So for the purpose of pursuing the subject, applied positive thinking, we will by-pass, and dismiss all of them. Rather, we will vigorously pursue the subject, power of positive thinking. Why? Because with that line of reasoning, one would believe that, the majority of reasonable thinkers would agree, **no one can be you, like you can be you.**

For the creationist thinker believes that mankind ____according to the creation story in Genesis already cited __ man was created "*in the image of God.*" Genesis 1:26. KJV. What does that mean? That we *look* like God? That we *think* and *talk* like God?

Many theologians hold to the thought that man was created to possess the characteristic or capabilities of God. That is, the ability to love God and others; to follow his teachings, i.e. "*Do unto others as you would have others do unto you;*" and to follow the Ten Commandments as a rule and guide for faith, and life, to include the ***applied power of positive thinking.***

And that man was created for a purpose; that purpose first of all, was to love God, and fellowship with God, and then to "*love one another.*" To "*...love your neighbor as you love yourself,*" Matthew 19:19 KJV, and to have fellowship (socialization) one with another. To marry and to be married: "*...for this cause (love) shall a man leave his father and mother and take unto him a wife...*" Matthew 19:5 KJV. (Paraphrase), and that, through that marriage union relationship pro-create a family: *"...multiply the earth."* Genesis 1:22 KJV.

The Bible asks the question: *"What is man that you (God) are mindful of him?"* Psalms 8:4 KJV. The answer is, God loves mankind (his creation) and wants only the best that life *has* to offer for his creation. *"And we know that all things work together for the good to those who love the Lord and are called according to his purpose."* Romans 8:28 KJV.

However, God will not do for man, what man is capable of accomplishing or doing for himself. In other words, when man does his best, God will take care of the rest.

This brings us full circle, back to the subject of the *applied power of positive thinking.* With the application of the power of positive thinking, plus faith to believe in one's self, accompanied by a providential source of reinforcement, man *can* achieve, consistent with the promise of Holy Scripture: *"I can do all things through Christ who gives me strength."* Philippians 4:13 KJV

Motivation, discussed in another chapter, is the catalyst that initiates *the applied power of positive thinking* and serves to bring about a successful conclusion or resolution. Motivation also initiates choice. The choice to apply the power of positive thinking is an individual choice.

Vignette:

The story is told of an old village wise man. He was so wise that all the residents of the village would bring their issues and problems to him for advice on a solution. Upon hearing their story the old wise man would sit down, bend over placing his elbows on his knees and with head in hand he would close his eyes and consider a solution to their problem. His advice was widely sought after because his suggestions for solution was never wrong, remarkably accurate and successful.

Some village teenagers were very jealous of the old wise man. They set about to trick him into giving *bad advice* so that they could prove him wrong. They contrived a plot to try and fool him.

One of the teenagers suggested a plan to the other two. It was agreed that they would take a canary from the cage of one of their mothers, seek out the old village wise man, stand before him and trick him. Holding the canary cupped in the hands of their leader they would ask him: *"is the canary alive or dead?"* If he replied dead, they would release the canary and have it fly away proving the old village wise man wrong. If he said alive, their leader would, with the strength of his hands, crush the canary to death and open his hands, showing that the canary was dead, proving the old village wise man to be wrong.

True to their plan they stood before the old village wise man, whereupon they asked their question: *"Is the canary alive or dead?"* Upon hearing their question the old wise man sat down, and bent over placing his elbows on his knees; with head in hand he closed his eyes and thoughtfully considered the question. Finally, he raised his head, looked the teenager directly in the eye and said, *"The choice is in your hands."*

So it is, the choice *is* in *your hands*. The wise choice; to facilitate **the applied power of positive thinking**.

CHAPTER 5

Be the BEST, You *Can* Be

There is an old cliché that says: *"Be the best you can be."* Nothing could be truer. Unfortunately, many people accept a lower standard than what they are capable of achieving. This is a tragedy. Another cliché says: *"I'm not perfect; no one else is perfect."* While this is the reality of truth, one can always strive to be better than a *minimal* performer.

For instance, let's take a work place environment. When an individual is given certain responsibility to perform a given task, whether it is an on-going, monotonous or repetitive task, there is always a better way to perform at that particular task. Again, in the work force, an axiom states: *"Go all the way, and then go the last mile; it is the last mile that counts."*

What is being said? The answer is obvious to many, but would be overlooked by some. So at the risk of insulting someone's intelligence, permit an explanation. When a person does only what is expected of them, by simply thinking this is all they pay me to do, it removes the challenge from the expected result level of performance result.

As an example, a carpenter can stand back at the end of the day, look at the work he accomplished during that day, and say, *"this is a worthwhile accomplishment."* On the other hand, an assembly line worker, at the end of the day, can find out from a supervisor what the level of their production during that day has been, and feel equally gratified with their level of achievement.

And while they are not able to visually see the result of their accomplishment, they can be equally satisfied in knowing that they have given a good day's work, for a good day's pay.

This method of evaluating one's level of performance can be rewarding and, at the same time, be self-satisfying in knowing that one has given their best in attempting to accomplish their goal of being the best they can be, at whatever they undertake.

Without equivocation this type of attitude strongly emphasizes *the applied power of positive thinking.*

There are two more areas which need to be discussed. They are, perseverance, (determination), and persistence (endurance).

Webster's dictionary defines perseverance as: *"patience and determination to achieve;"* persistence is defined as: *"endurance; to persevere in spite of obstacles."*

Obviously, without either perseverance or persistence one cannot be fully successful in obtaining their goals. Someone has said, *"A bird in the hand is worth two in the bush."*

The thought being, anything you set your mind to can realistically be achieved (within reason). Quite obviously, *the applied power of positive thinking* will not, *repeat*, will not cause you to become a million dollar lottery winner. There is a great difference between *realistic*, and *"pie in the sky, by and by"* thinking.

There is no *known* historical record for achievement ever having been successfully accomplished by simply *wishing* for, or *hoping* for, some task to be performed successfully.

Someone has said, *"There is no elevator to success; you have to take the stairs."*

Success comes through careful planning, hard work, effort, determination and unswerving perseverance. Combine all of these elements and they spell out a powerful dynamic; ***the applied power of positive thinking.***

CHAPTER 6

Setting Goals: Immediate (Short-term); Median, and Long Range

The average person has not thought about, nor planned for goal setting. The majority of people go from one day to the next all of their life. There is a saying that holds true for many people:

"*Work 8 to 5 until your 65*," or longer, in today's down-turned economy.

It doesn't have to be that way. How can it be avoided? This is a valid and credible question. The answer is *not* that complex.

Whether you are an unskilled day laborer, or a CEO Executive, planning is an essential part of living a positive and successful life, filled with achievements. In order to have a plan an individual must necessarily know what they want out of life. This is a goal in itself. Once that intended goal mind set has been established, the goal setting can begin. Here is where *the applied power of positive thinking* comes into focus.

THE IMMEDIATE (Short-term) GOAL:

If you are a day laborer, and your goal is to become a skilled worker, then certain mini-goals must be set and worked toward. This would be considered a "short-term goal" which could be achieved in 12 to 18 months. To move from an unskilled day laborer to a skilled worker an individual must necessarily obtain training. So it would appear that the logical action to take would be to enroll in either an ROP (in California – Regional Occupational Program), or enroll in community college training programs consistent with the new intended skilled occupation, i.e. electrical, auto mechanic, computer technician technology, etc. With the proper skilled training background an immediate, (short-term) goal can be readily doable, and obtainable.

This type performance would satisfy the suggestion for setting and reaching a (short-term) immediate goal. In the truest sense, this positive action would be considered a clear-cut example of *how* to facilitate **the applied the power of positive thinking**.

THE MEDIAN (Mid-range) GOAL

While there is no *specific* time frame measured in months or years for achieving goals, it is reasonable to set a time frame for achievement. This time frame not only dictates the length of time an individual will take to reach a specific goal, it also inspires and motivates positive action toward obtaining the goal. A reasonable time frame for the median goal, while not set in stone, would be from 18 to 36 months.

Again, the length of time to reach a specific goal would be dependent upon available educational possibilities offered in community colleges or other available training programs.

Getting started toward reaching a set goal is a major hurdle. Unfortunately, too many persons procrastinate about getting started. Obviously, this pushes the attainment of the set goal farther and farther away and may impact an individual's opportunity and possibility of ever getting started.

This is influence by the negative aspect, and for the purpose of this work would be unacceptable. Rather, it is the intent of the writer to keep in focus *the applied power of positive thinking*.

The not so obvious benefit, of setting a median goal, is so that when the short-term goal is successfully reached, then the stimuli for attaining the median goal stimulates thinking, and creates motivation to start working toward achieving the next goal.

Someone has said, *"If you don't have a target, you will achieve just what you shoot at… nothing."* This mind set is also reinforced by the words of another who said, *"He who has little or no expectations, is never disappointed."* The point: expect nothing; receive nothing: shooting at no target, obviously, will achieve… nothing.

To recap what has been said, when a short-term goal has been achieved, one can immediately start working on the achievement of a median range goal. Once the median range goals has been achieved, then immediate work can begin on the long range goal.

THE LONG RANGE (Long-term) GOAL:

The long term, or long range, goal would expectantly have a realistic time frame of 3 to 5 years. If this appears unrealistic, just know that a lot of effort, energy, and time have been invested in putting forth the energy to achieve both the short term and median range goals.

Perhaps one of the strongest enemies against goal achievement is unrealistic expectations by the individual setting the goals. Unrealistic expectations produce anxiety, frustration, discouragement, and disappointment to the point of believing that the goal cannot be reached.

In turn, these frustrations often lead to giving up the quest for goal achievement. By staying focused on achievement of the intended goal an individual stays motivated and can, through perseverance achieve any realistic goal.

In the course of obtaining achievement for the long range goal the individual needs to immediately establish another set of goals. That is, short term, median range, and long term goals.

Vignette:

There is a story in a children's book about a little train. In the story the train is challenged to chug up. and around a mountain. As the little train begins it journey up the mountain side it begins to express an attitude: *"I think I can; I think I can, I think I can..."* gaining speed, and confidence. the little trains moves faster and more confidently around the pathway leading up, and around the mountain. Halfway up the mountain the little train gains additional speed, and even more confidence, and expresses a reinforced and stronger attitude: *"I know I can; I know I can; I know I can..."* and confidently glided around the mountain all the way to the very top shouting, *"I can; I can; I did!"* The little train's short term goal (I think I can); the median term goal (I know I can), and long term goal (I can; I can,; I did), had all been achieved.

This method for setting and achieving goals keeps the individual's mind alert, sharp, focused, and on the cutting edge, for superior goal achievement through the *applied* power of positive thinking.

Goal summary:

When the author speaks the word "goal" it is not "pie in the sky, by and by" thinking.

It is *Goal Specific*; specificity, to use another term, i.e. using certain dynamics for goal setting.

The goal dynamics are:

S ='s	**SPECIFIC**
M ='s	**MEASURABLE**
A ='s	**ATTAINABLE**
R ='s	**REALISTIC**
T ='s	**TIME BOUND** (Time Frame for Achieving)

Each of these dynamics will be briefly discussed:

S ='s SPECIFIC   In order for a "goal" to be successfully achievable **it** has to be specific, i.e. you need to have a plan. There is an old saying which states: *"have a plan; work the plan."* The thought being, select the objective "goal" and work toward that goal.

For example, if your "goal" is to pursue and earn a degree from a university, and you are working full time, the specific goal would be to earn the degree. Obviously, working full time precludes enrolling as a full time student. Therefore, it will be necessary to set a goal of taking one course of study at a time, either in evening classes or on line, until all of the requirements have been met to earn the degree.

This goal would fall into **THE LONG RANGE (Long-term)** category; it qualifies as a particular goal and would be expected to have a realistic time frame for achievement of 3 to 5 years.

M ='s MEASURABLE   A measurable goal presents a dynamic which can be realistically measured as progress proceeds along the time line for achievement.

That is to say, the measurable goal would exhibit *progressive achievement toward goal completion.*

For example:

Jane has a goal of becoming a beautician. She has set a time frame of eighteen months, to two years for achievement.

This time frame includes completion of the course work instruction (*twelve months*); completion of the practicum – i.e. hands on training (*six months*), application for the state board and waiting time (*three months*), taking the state board examination (*one month*), waiting time (*two months*) from the state board notification of examination pass/fail.

Assuming Jane passed the state board, she makes application for state licensure (one month), and wait time for receipt of state licenses, Jane now becomes a state licensed beautician.

Realistically, Jane has been able to appropriately measure her goal progress, at every step of achievement, and to obtain her goal in twenty-four months; right on target and well within the goal achievement time frame.

THE IMMEDIATE (Short-term) GOAL:

A ='s	**ATTAINABLE**
R ='s	**REALISTIC**
T ='s	**TIME BOUND** (Time Frame for Achieving)

For the immediate, short-term goal two of the dynamics are going to be dealt with simultaneously; they fit together like hand and glove. For successful achievement these two dynamics have to be realistic. One cannot be achieved without the other .Obviously, any goal has be measured by both of these dynamics. By the same token if a goal is not realistic, neither can it be achieved.

This sounds like juvenile language but, believe it or not, there are many people who strive to achieve an impossible goal and subsequently, pursue an impossible dream.

If a goal is not attainable or doable then it cannot be achieved; it is that simple, regardless of how much positive thinking is applied.

For instance, if a person has a goal of becoming rich, just because that person keeps on buying lottery tickets doesn't realistically put them any closer to becoming a lottery winner and becoming a millionaire; enough said.

As has previously been stated the immediate or "short-term goal" could realistically be achieved in 12 to 18 months.

For example:

John was an engineer with a national aerospace company. Due to downsizing he was laid off. John has not been able to find comparable employment; John has been unemployed for two years. Discouraged and disappointed by being out of work and not having any prospects for employment from sending out resumes, he has now vowed to set a goal to become re-employed within eighteen months.

In view of his new found goal the first thing John does is to take his resume to a professional resume service provider and have the resume updated and reworked. He then devotes 4 hours a day, from 8 Am to 12 noon, to reading want ads and responding with a resume.

He also goes on the Web and places his resume with every major head-hunter agency and professional job placement agency.

This was a repeat of what John had already done when he had initially been laid off, however, he had not received any tangible job offers with the "old" resume. His previous efforts had received little or no positive results.

John's revised resume now contained language he had not used in the old resume. The statement was, *"willing to work out of the area or to relocate."* A statement John had not even considered prior to this time.

Within three months of posting his resume on line and with employment agencies John had received 3 offers for employment comparable to the work he had been laid off from. All the offers were for employment out of town.

In six months' time John was again fully employed in a position that was 60 miles from his home. A small sacrifice having to communicate 60 miles each way, or 120 miles per day, considering that he had been unemployed for the past 24 months.

This is a valid example of how determination combined with a realistic, doable immediate goal can be achieved. John had met his immediate, short-term goal ahead of the time line schedule he had set for obtainment.

Each of these examples, strongly demonstrate how setting realistic, doable, attainable goals _ whether short-term, mid-term, or long-range _ *can* produce positive results when facilitated by **the *applied* power of positive *thinking,***

CHAPTER 7

PMA – Positive Mental Attitude; Image Setting

There is an old expression which says, *"Believe in something, or you will fall for anything."* This is especially true when a person considers their individual options in life. For example, when one gets up in the morning, looks out the window, and sees that it is day light their response can either be: *"Good Lord, it's morning!"* Or conversely, *"Good morning, Lord."*

What the author likes to refer to as the early morning *"wake-up call"* sets the attitudinal tone and mood for the day. One can be happy; one can be sad; one can be positive, or one can be negative.

There is no middle ground. The *"wake-up call"* thought process sets the mood for the rest of the day. So *why not* have PMA, positive mental attitude?

This early on attitude also sets the image of one's self. For instance, the mind set can be strongly influenced by the power of positive thinking, i.e. *"I'm going to be very successful today, on the job in my work, and in dealing with others. I will perform at the highest level I am capable of performing at, and I will accomplish much."*

And further stating, *"I am going to get in touch with my seeds of greatness and rise to a new level in my performance, beyond employer expectation."*

On the other hand, an unsuccessful image can also be strongly influenced by negative thought, i.e. *"I don't feel very good today. I don't know if I want to go to work or not. No one will miss me. Besides, everyone else takes sick leave, why shouldn't I? If you don't use it, you lose it. Well, maybe I will go to work, but I am just going to coast today. I will only do what is expected of me, like everyone else. It's only a job, and if they fire me, so what? I was looking for a job when I found this one."*

IMAGE SETTING:

The majority of people in society today do not have a clue on image setting. In other words, they have no idea of what position they currently occupy in life, nor do they know how to imagine what they want to be.

This is a tragedy; it stands to reason that, if a person doesn't know where they are, then how can they know where they are going, or where they want to be, and what do they want to achieve in life?

Subsequently, if in fact you are unhappy in your present life mode, and you hold an image of yourself in low self-esteem, then how *can* you change that image to become happy and positive? It is impossible unless you know how to change your image. To illustrate, let's review several example scenarios.

EXAMPLE 1:

Let's assume you are now thirty years old, male or female (it doesn't matter) and you are still single. In your mind's eye you have always thought of yourself as one day being married, and a parent with a family. However, you have never been able to find a "Mr. or Miss Right." Although you have met several persons with whom you have seriously considered a marital relationship, it has never seemed to work out. Therefore, in your own view you have a failed image and see yourself as a loser in the arena of marriage. How do you change that image?

EXAMPLE 2:

You have been married for ten years, have a loving, compatible mate, and for whatever reason, have not been able to have a family. Both you and your spouse have been medically examined and have not been diagnosed with particular reason, *as to why*, there has never been a pregnancy. Perhaps each of you has adopted the image of remaining childless. How can you change that image, and what can be done to produce a family

EXAMPLE 3:

You are a would-be grandparent and have an only child; a married daughter. All of your adult parent life you have had an image, of your daughter having children and of you being a grandparent. To your dismay, and great disappointment, this has not happened and your daughter has now been successfully married for seven years. You are told that a decision has been made by them not to have any children. Your mind is saddened, and your heart is broken at the thought of never being a grandparent. How can you change your thinking to use as a vehicle to alter your image so you can again have a happy life?

Hypothetical synopses will be used illustrating how you *can change* your image for fulfillment to a happy life.

First, let's explore the dynamics of Example Number 1, the single, thirty year old. This appears to be a clear cut dynamic of unrealized expectation. Perhaps a case of unrealistic expectations. The scenario is: a desire to be married; having met several persons with whom you have seriously considered a marital relationship, but it has never seemed to work out. Therefore, in your own view you have a failed image, and see yourself as a loser in the arena of marriage.

The question is, why did none of the relationships evolve into marriage? What was, and is, your expectation? Of course, everyone is looking for the "perfect" mate. When you use a yardstick as a measurement for the word "perfect" what measure are you using?

Too many people want a "perfect" mate measured in the eyes of the world: a number 10, for a female; that is, a beautiful (female), with perfect measurements; and the proverbial tall, dark and very handsome person for a male. Since, in the eyes of the world no one is perfect, this is unrealistic expectations and, therefore, they never appear to "measure up" to the worlds and, subsequently, *your* expectation.

Conversely, in the realistic eyes of humanity, it should be a foregone conclusion that, since no one is "perfect," your expectation has to change. In order to climb aboard a vehicle that will transport you to a happy life, your image must also change. That is, I am not perfect, therefore, I will accept someone else who does not necessarily measure up to the level of my unrealistic expectations. In so doing, my unrealistic expectations are met at the level of reality and subsequently promotes change in attitude and thinking.

As a result of applying the power of positive thinking the mind set changes, expectation becomes more focused and realistic, and goals more doable and attainable. Thus, meeting that someone who does now measure up to your level of expectation becomes realistic.

In other words, you become less choosy and critical of someone from the opposite sex whom you would consider marrying, And one day it happens; you meet someone who steals away your heart!

Vignette:

Carol was not an attractive girl, neither was she homely. She had a pug nose, a high forehead, and slightly protruding front teeth. In her own eyes she thought that, according to the world's standard, she was ugly. Carol never gave up hope. She kept telling herself, "one day."

In high school, her attractive girl friends were always the ones to be asked out on dates. In college, she had been asked to be a bridesmaid in a couple of her friend's weddings. She begin to believe that this would always be her role in a wedding; always a bridesmaid, never a bride.

Upon graduating from college she went to work for a law firm where she met a new law graduate who had just been admitted to the bar. His name was Charlie. She was so busy getting her feet on the ground with the law firm with whom she worked ____ and where he also was now a junior attorney ____ that she didn't give him a second thought. The same was not to be said about Junior attorney Charles L. Knight, II. He was assigned an office adjacent to Carol's. She helped him set up the new office. Why not? She asked herself, which appeared to be one of her jobs as Assistant Executive Secretary.

Once Charles was settled into his office he seemed to find ways to approach Carol about the smallest of issues. For instance he asked her if she was a "pool secretary," or did she work "for one particular Senior Attorney?" If he needed to dictate a letter, how did he go about getting it typed? etc. She patiently explained answers to his questions, trying to always remain courteous and professional and, that's not all, she consoled herself, he was "kind of cute."

Charles did not make it a secret that he was pursuing Carol. It wasn't long before he was asking her to lunch with him in the executive tower cafeteria, asking her to go out with him, and always ready to pay her a compliment. Carol was flattered but wasn't sure it was wise to date or associate with a fellow employee, even though he was a junior executive in the firm. She had observed other secretaries going out with some of the senior attorney's and learned that there was no company policy or rule against it. Still, she hesitated. Attorney Charles would not give up. He continued to ask her out. Finally, she accepted his invitation. They went to dinner and the theater and enjoyed a wonderful evening. In six months they were dating steadily. Carol was elated and wondered why she had not accepted Charles's invitation earlier.

Carol and Charles dated for over a year before things got serious. A causal relationship turned romantic. Charles asked her to marry him; she accepted. They set a date, he gave her a ring, and they started planning a wedding. Carol later said, that she had to "pinch herself almost daily" to remind her that this was really happening.

The date they set to be married coincided with the two year anniversary of their first meeting. Their plan was to be married and honeymoon in Hawaii.

It is reported by friends that, at last contact, Carol and Charles have been married for three years. She is in the fourth month of a first pregnancy.

Not bad for someone who believed, just a few short years ago, that she was "ugly" and that her role in a wedding would always "be only a bridesmaid, never a bride."

This is another crystal clear example, for accomplishment caused, at least in part, by *the applied power of positive thinking.*

Now let' consider Example Number 2:

You have been married for ten years, have a loving, compatible mate, and for whatever reason, have not been able to have a family. Both you and your spouse have been medically examined and have not been diagnosed with any particular medical reason, as to why, there has never been a pregnancy

The underlying question would be: Do you each continue to want children? If so, what alternatives and options are you willing to consider?

If your answer to question number one is "Yes," then you are ready to consider viable and credible option alternatives. What are those available options?

First, there is the option for adoption. Secondly, there is the option for Foster Care.

Each of those options will be briefly described:

ADOPTION:

Definition: Adoption by definition is the act of transferring parent(s) rights to an adoptive Parent or parents. Adoption is the legal procedure where birth parents relinquish their rights to a biological child to N adoptive parent or parents, who in turn, legally assume the role of parent(s) for a child(person), usually under the age of 18 years, who is not their biological offspring.

The adopted child (person) becomes a full and legal member of the adoptive family and is entitled to the same legal status privileges as the adoptive parents biographical children, (if any).

FIVE TYPES OF ADOPTION:

There are basically five types of adoption. They are *Domestic, Open, Closed, Tran racial,* and *International* Adoptions. Within the framework of the adoption procedure there is other dynamics such as special needs adoptive children, relative adoption, such as grandparents, celebrity adoption, and others. This work is neither intended to advise, suggest, or to be statistically definitive. The intent is for information only. For that purpose only the basic adoption types and definitions will be briefly stated and discussed

Domestic Adoption: Under this term domestic adoption is usually considered to be within the confines of the United States, and more explicitly, within particular states. Each state have their own laws and procedures, and rules in place. To find out what the laws, procedures and rules are, one simply has to conduct a web search under their state name and adoptions.

Open Adoptions: This term refers to an open relationship and exchange of information between birth parents and adoptive parents. The relationship continues through the adoption process and remains intact through the post-adoptive years and may include visitation by the birth parents.

Closed Adoption: The closed adoption term describes no established and / or existing relationship between the birth parents and the adoptive parents. Under the terms of closed adoptions parents usually keep the information related to their adoption from the child until he / she becomes an adult. Some adoptive parents never tell their adopted child about their adoption, to protect them from the trauma of finding out that they are not biological. However, today, research indicates many adoptive parents do tell their adopted children as early as possible about their adoption. Thus, attempting to avoid any later-life psychological issues that may be related to their adoption

Tran racial Adoptions: The definition of a tranracial adoption is when the adopted Child (ren) come from a different ethnic culture, and are of a different race than their adoptive parents. Tran racial adoption appears to be coming more common in the United States, perhaps due to the availability of different cultures and race of adoptive children, and also may be due to being promulgated by publicity of celebrity adoptions, (international adoptions: to be discussed later), and the availability of special needs children.

International Adoption: The definition of international adoption is, adopting a child, or children, from a foreign country. The United States leads every other nation in the world for the majority of international adoptions. The second greatest majority is European followed by other more developed countries. International adoption laws vary and are more difficult in different in nations. Other countries are more willing to cooperate with international adoptions and have definitive, and well established laws, procedures and rules to follow. At least one country, the United Arab Emirates (UAE), forbids international adoptions.

Foster Care / Adoption: Foster Care Parenting is where, under the direction of the state, adult parents care for minor children who are not able to live with their biological parents. While Foster Care is not adoption *per se*, in America, many adoptive children are placed through the foster care system.

According to Wikipedia, the free encyclopedia, with enactment of the Adoption and Safe Families Act of 1997, the number of children adopted from foster care in the United States has approximately doubled.

It again needs to be stated that, this work is not intended to set forth statistics, or to be statistically correct and / or definitive regarding laws, rules and regulations for the United States or other countries. It is provided for information only; the information presented was accurate at the time this work was written.

There are many websites available in reference to adoption. The websites offer copious information for those who may be considering adoption, or for those who may be interested in learning more about adoptions, or foster care procedures. The websites list agencies, various state laws, rules and regulations applicable to particular states concerning adoption. Each state has their own adoption laws, rules, and regulations in place. Some of those website addresses are listed at the end of this chapter.

It is the intent of the author, that by providing this informative information, the essence of adoption has been captured. For couples who remain parentless, but want children __ and still hold forth a desire to become parents __ the options are realistic, and opportunities are unlimited.

To coin a phrase, *"The journey of a thousand miles, begins with the first step."* There are numerous, unlimited opportunities for childless couples who want children to become adoptive parents. Obviously, the choice remains with the would-be parents.

Subsequently, the applied power of positive thinking is again proved. Childless couples, who want to be parents, can become happy, productive parents and can achieve their dream.

The formula for producing miracles: Desire, combined with facilitation of ***the applied power of positive thinking.***

Vignette: An Adoptive Couple

Marsha and Steve dated for two years before getting serious about marriage. They followed a pattern set by numerous young adults. That is, living together for awhile, to see if they were compatible, before fully committing to a permanent marital relationship.

For Marsha and Steve it appeared to have worked out. The two years of living together seemed to have solidified their compatibility, and they had learned to disagree agreeably and successfully massage personality differences.

They now believed they could build a very successful marriage. One major difference was still unresolved; Steve wanted children, but Marsha was unable to bear children due to a severe childhood illness. Subsequently, their some time discussions concerning children usually ended in a stalemate. They agreed to deal with the subject after they were married.

They set a date for the wedding and excitedly looked forward to a honeymoon in Hawaii. The big day arrived, and the families of both participated in the wedding, and reception. They wished them happiness and pleasure as they left for their honeymoon.

A week after the honeymoon they returned to their daytime jobs: He as a system analyst programmer for a major university, and she to the hospital where she was employed as a fulltime registered nurse.

In the fairyland world of Oz, it would end by saying they lived happily ever after. But in the reality of the here and now, it didn't work out that way. Steve was one of seven adult children and he often spoke of feeling cheated by not being able to become a father. The more he talked about it to Marsha, the unhappier he appeared to be.

Due to the stress of their high profile employment, coupled with the dissatisfaction of being childless began to put a strain on their marriage.

They both realized that if they didn't make an attempt at resolution, with regard to the childless dilemma, the strain could ultimately cause a crack to appear in their new marital relationship. They privately discussed the situation at length and decided to seek counsel from each of their employee assistance programs consultants.

At first, they each met individually with their referred marriage / family counselors, and then conjointly. They were fortunate in being referred to therapists who had both education and experience in dealing with childless couples.

It appears as if their referral therapists had received some divine guidance: both of the therapists, without consulting with one another, recommended they consider and explore the possibility of adoption, or foster parenting.

It has been said that *"sometimes the obvious bites us."* It began to seem that way to Marsha and Steve. It appeared to be such a simple solution; adoption __ a subject they had briefly discussed during their pre-marriage, trial relationship __ and yet, had not come back into focus after their marriage. They were both embarrassed and elated.

With the assistance of an adoption agency of choice they began the adoption application procedure. It was their desire to adopt a new-born, without regard to gender, and thus began a rather lengthy process of meeting the required qualification.

After many interviews, personality, testing, and compatibility tests they were adoption approved. Within ten months after starting the application process, having reviewed several adoptive new-born they finally received the perfect match. They became adoptive parents of a beautiful 7 pound 9 ounce baby girl; Gloria.

This is yet another example of how miraculous circumstances are influenced by application of the power of positive thinking.

A REVERSE, NEGATIVE / POSITIVE:

Now, let's consider a reverse negative/positive. John and Joan had been married for eleven years. They had married late in life; he had been 45 and she had been ten years younger at 35. Each of them loved children, and were at the time of marriage looking forward to having children, but although they had tried, they never produced any children as a result of their union.

Although they were disappointed, it was resolved in their own minds that they were not going to become biological parents. Neither were they interested in adoption or foster care. Still, they continued to love, and to be around children. They were devoted Christians and decided to explore ways in which they could be active with children. They went to the leader of their church and explained their interest. It was suggested to them that they become active in the church nursery, and to also consider becoming teachers in the church school. John and Joan did what had been suggested. Joan volunteered in the (bed-baby) infant nursery and John volunteered to work with the toddlers.

By so doing both Joan and John were able to satisfy their desire to be with children and to share their love. Ten years have passed and both Joan and John have found great fulfillment in their volunteer work. They remain very active teaching in the church school and volunteering in the church nursery.

Joan and John, challenged by a negative situation, appropriately applied the power of positive thinking turning the negative into a positive. Recognizing that they would never be biological parents they pursued and captured their dream of sharing their love for, and with children by being volunteer, surrogate parents.

This is another example of how *desired* and *positive* end results can be successfully achieved , under seemingly impossible circumstances and situations, by facilitating ***the applied power of positive thinking.***

Most Popular Websites: Copyright 2013 Elevati, LLC

Adoption.com - #1 adoption site
Adoption.org – adoption neighborhood
Adopting.org – friendly adoption support and & information
123Adoption - basic adoption info on hundreds of topics
AdoptionInformation.com - your guide to adoption on the internet
123Adoption Sister Sites - adoption, parenting, foster, pregnancy, etc

Local Adoption

State Adoptions - basic state adoption info
Alabama Adoption | Alaska Adoption | Arizona Adoption | Arkansas Adoption | California Adoption | Colorado Adoption | Connecticut Adoption | Delaware Adoption | District of Columbia Adoption | Florida Adoption | Georgia Adoption | Hawaii Adoption | Idaho Adoption | Illinois Adoption | Indiana Adoption | Iowa Adoption | Kansas Adoption | Kentucky Adoption | Louisiana Adoption | Maine Adoption | Maryland Adoption | Massachusetts Adoption | Michigan Adoption | Minnesota Adoption | Mississippi Adoption | Missouri Adoption | Montana Adoption | Nebraska Adoption | Nevada Adoption | New Hampshire Adoption | New Jersey Adoption | New Mexico Adoption | New York Adoption | North Carolina Adoption | North Dakota Adoption | Ohio Adoption | Oklahoma Adoption | Oregon Adoption | Pennsylvania Adoption | Rhode Island Adoption | South Carolina Adoption | South Dakota Adoption | Tennessee Adoption | Texas Adoption | Utah Adoption | Vermont Adoption | Virginia Adoption | Washington Adoption | Washington DC Adoption | West Virginia Adoption | Wisconsin Adoption | Wyoming Adoption

Professionals

Adoption Directory – largest directory of adoption agencies, professionals and services
Adoption Professionals - online resource center & networking only for adoption professionals
Adoption Counselors – tips on selecting an adoption counselor
Adoption Yellow Pages –internet's yellow pages for adoption professionals
Adoption Jobs – find an adoption job or post your job openings
Find Professionals - information on finding an adoption professional
For Professionals - resources for adoption professionals
FamilyAds.com - cost-effective adoption advertising solutions

Foster Care

<u>Foster Parenting</u> - largest foster care site with thousands of pages
<u>Foster Care</u> - basic info on foster care
<u>Foster Forums</u> - foster care message boards

CHAPTER 8

Positive vs. Negative

Negative influences are all around us. We often hear people proclaiming, "You can't do that!" in response to hearing someone say that they are going to do a seemingly impossible task.

Subsequently, if we listen to the naysayers, and repeat that phrase to ourselves enough times, we ultimately convince ourselves that seeming impossible tasks cannot be accomplished.

It would be an understatement to say and, or believe that negative though *is not* very powerful. Indeed, it is.

As an illustration, let's take an example shared with me by a colleague I was visiting with years ago.

This colleague, a male, had a broken tail light. It happened to be the glass over the stop light was cracked and part of it had fallen away. He was very aware of the broken light, and fully intended to have it repaired, however, due to his busy schedule he had never gotten around to it.

Each time he drove the vehicle he reminded himself of the broken tail light and silently told himself that he was probably going to get stopped and get a ticket. He was not disappointed.

Within a month from the time the light was broken he was driving home one day and noticed a police car turning a corner into his lane behind him. The thought about the broken tail light popped into his mind and he again said to himself, this cop is probably going to stop me and write me a ticket. Almost immediately he saw a red light come on behind him. He pulled to the curb, and tried to pleasantly greet the police officer. The officer asked for his driver's license, registration and insurance, and then asked. *"Do you know why I stopped you?"* My colleague said, *"To be perfectly honest, it's probably because of the broken tail light."* *"Bingo!"* The officer replied. *"How long has the light been broken?"* he continued. *"About a month now,"* my colleague told him. *"I'm going to write you a fix-it ticket. It will not be a fine. How soon can you have it repaired?"* he asked. *"This coming Saturday,"* my colleague replied. *"I'm going to give you fifteen days to get it fixed. After the repair you can go to any police department and have an officer sign off on it, and the ticket will be satisfied,"* the officer told my friend

This may appear to be juvenile and nonsensical to some. However, call it what you will, it is a proven fact that *negativity attracts negativity*.

Permit another similar example and illustration that will prove the opposite; that positivity attracts positive results. Another friend, who was, at the time, a police officer. He had a jeep vehicle he rarely drove but the license registration had expired. Since he always planned to sell the vehicle he never re-registered the vehicle, and neither did he ever apply for a non-usage permit. Yet, to keep the vehicle in working order, until he got around to selling it, he would on occasion drive it on the street. Each time he drove it he emptied his mind to the fact that the license registration was expired and that he was in violation by driving the vehicle. This went on for the four years that I knew him and he was never stopped, and never received a citation. Juvenile, ridiculous, nonsensical, you say. Enough said; the point is proved. Negativity *attracts negativity*; positivity produces positive results.

Beyond these two examples and illustrations there is more to be said about negativity vs. positivity. For example the author remembers a time when working as an executive consultant for a firm that was bought by another company. The sale of the company happened at the end of March and became effective April 1st. The writer received a W-2 Wage Income for the new company but, for whatever reason no W-2 Wage Earned Income Form was received from the old company for the first three months of the year. Without thinking income taxes were filed only on the new company against the wages earned for only nine months. However the original company had forwarded the wages I had earned for the first three month to the IRS. Shortly after filing my income tax for the year I was contacted via letter by the IRS and advised that I had not declared the reported income earned from the original company.

My first response was panic; I realized the massive amount of interest levied by the IRS on past due income. I immediately contacted the IRS agent whose name appeared on the letter and explained the circumstances. I was advised to have my *"accountant submit a revised Income Tax Return within thirty days"* and, since income tax had been held from the unreported wages, that *"the late payment penalty would be waived; that I would have to pay only any additional taxes due."*

Regardless of *who* you are, as to age, your position, income, or life status, to receive a letter from the IRS advising that *"there is a discrepancy in your income tax filing"* it has the potential of sending a cold chill up your spine. The original letter from the IRS simply stated that there had been *"a discrepancy,"* and that I should *"contact the IRS Agent at once."*

I received this notice on a Saturday so I had the entire week-end to wonder what *"the discrepancy"* was. However, being a positive person I simply applied the power of positive thinking, and lo and behold, the positive thought paid off. As I recall, the amount due and payable on the increased income was just a few hundred dollars, and the good part was that there was no penalty interest.

Yet another example of positive results brought about through facilitation of **the applied power of positive thinking.**

CHAPTER 9

Stress: Living With, OR Without

Medical statistics document that stress is the major cause of heart attacks and that heart attacks continue to be the number one killer of adult men and women in the United States.

Medical science also demonstrates that a certain amount of stress is very normal and, in fact, good. Physicians testify that low levels of stress help to hone the senses and assist in activating the mind to a keener and sharper focus on the task at hand.

Yet, excess stress raises the blood pressure and elevates the anxiety level, speeds up the heart rate and raises the adrenalin causing an exacerbation of extreme elevated stress levels, dangerously high blood pressure and high anxiety. High blood pressure has been medically identified as "the silent killer." Why? Because stress is linked to both physical and mental health and can slowly overtake one's life to the point of death.

Stress can be defined as the daily wear and tear on both the body and mind in everyday life, coming from both *external* and *internal* sources.

Stress exhibits itself in at least four different dynamics. They are:

1. **Acute Stress**: It exhibits through agitation and pressure, emotional upsets, and gastrointestinal disturbances

2. **Chronic Stress**: Is the most serious kind of stress. It is identified as "never ending Stress." It hammers away at the mind and body and drives down resistance. It contributes to diseases such as cancer, diabetes, and decreased and compromised immune competence

3. **Acute Stress – Episodic**: Exhibits through anxiety, depression, migraines, heart attack, hypertension, serious gastrointestinal distress and cardiovascular accident (stroke)

4. **Traumatic Stress**: Resulting from massive acute stress and is very difficult to reduce. Post-Traumatic Stress disorder can be attributed to Traumatic Stress.

Statistically, it is reported that "job burnout" alone is experienced by 25% to 40% of the United States working population and that, $300 billion, or $7,500 per worker is spent per year in the United States on stress-related health insurance compensation claims health costs.

Multiple health problems are also linked to stress, and stress contributes to the leading cause of death in the United States for accidents, cancer, cirrhosis of the liver, heart disease, lung disease, and suicide.

Medical science identify three dynamics that relate to achieving and maintaining good health. They are: proper diet, along with eating fruits and vegetables; exercise (walking is one of the best types of exercise), and rest. It has been medically determined that the average adult needs between 7 to 9 hours of rest and sleep.

This work is not intended to offer medical advice. The medical dynamics mentioned is either recent medically documented statistics, or well know medical facts, which can be verified on the world wide web. The intent in mentioning these dynamics in a general sense is simply to attest to the fact that the formula for achieving and maintaining good health is not monopolized by prescription drugs, surgeries, vitamins and health clubs. Rather, good health is obtained and maintained through conscientious knowledge, desire, directed effort, common sense, the power of applied thinking and stick-to-itiveness; a combination of all the above. Realistically, it is an impossibility to enjoy a stress-free mind set without a healthy body.

How *can* a stress filled life to be avoided? First and foremost, the mind has to be emptied of anxiety, doubt, uncertainty, indeciviness and lack of self-confidence. One must have a solid foundation; you can't build a house on a foundation of sand or over a swamp. In like manner, one cannot build a strong, healthy, trouble and stress-free foundation on a mind filled with uncertainty, and indeciviness. Rather, the mind foundation must be solidly built on a strong, unshakeable foundational power of applied positive thought. It is reported that more than 50% of Americans suffer adverse health effects due to stress.

Medical researchers estimate that up to 90% of illness and disease is stress related, and is linked to the most common causes of death, i.e. accidents, cancer, cirrhosis of the liver, heart disease, and suicide,

This reasoning will be further discussed - in vignettes - to illustrate and demonstrate the effect of stress examples of workable solutions to remarkably reduce, and in some cases, eliminate major stress through the power of applied positive thinking.

Vignette:

John Drake, a 34 year-old sales executive, learned to balance his daily work-life after he experienced "heart attack" symptoms.

John was chief sales director for an aggressive state-of-the-art, high-tech firm. At age 34 he was being considered for promotion to Vice President of Sales. His current position was fast-moving with heavy demands. When he learned of his pending promotion the stress he was already experiencing became even more acute. He recognized that he should be pacing himself to help relieve some of the stress but he consoled himself by thinking I'm young, healthy and in control of his life. He assured himself he could "handle the stress."

While on the outside he didn't exhibit noticeable signs of stress, on the inside, he felt like the wheels of his employment train was about to come off the track. In his innermost mind he realized he was a bundle of nerves. He had been having episodes of chest pain, dizziness, shortness of breath, and heart palpitations. Sometimes he felt like he was going to pass out which caused him to become anxious to the point of panic. What worried him most was that these panic attacks could strike without reason or warning.

The panic attack symptoms were so severe that on several occasions he was rushed by Paramedics to a nearby hospital emergency room; he feared that he was having a heart attack. In the ER he was informed that tests revealed nothing wrong with his heart.

However, he remained convinced that he had been on the verge of a heart attack. He scheduled an appointment with a cardiologist who conducted a battery of tests with no remarkable physical findings. The cardiologist observed how stressed John was and suggested a change of life-style.

John wondered how he could change his life style. He worked from 7 AM until 12 Midnight 7 days a week and it had paid off; he was being considered for a vice president position. But as he thought about his responsibilities he recognized that for his efforts – though they had been recognized by higher management – he had paid a physical price.

In spite of all the negative tests he still believed he had come very close to having a heart attack.

He continued to think about how he could slow down his pace and protect his health. He knew he had an "A" Type personality, but he also knew that he never said "No" to a senior executive who wanted an additional job done, like setting up financial budgets for his department – when in reality, that should have been the treasurers' responsibility; or, of setting up work schedules and projected budgets for his, and other departments, when that should have been the responsibility of the supervisor in each department.

He slowly came to the conclusion, even at the risk of losing a promotion, he had to learn how to start saying *"No."*

That is *exactly* what he did. To his surprise, rather than lose respect - by refusing to take on additional responsibilities – respect for him actually increased, and he did, in fact, receive the promotion to Vice President of Sales. He cut his work week to 5 days, from 8 AM 'til 5 PM, and started spending more time with his wife and two children on week-ends, started using his membership at the Fitness Club by working out several times a week. He began to see a very real difference in his overall physical feeling, and was able to have some quality peace of mind.

The exercise paid off by helping him to get rid of a double-chin, and to flatten out his stomach, which was beginning to protrude over his belt. In just six months of a changed life-style he had lost fifteen pounds; he never felt better.

John achieved the results through a changed attitude and determination, combined with t*he power of applied positive thinking.*

Another crystal clear example of how a proven *formula* can bring about desired, positive end results by facilitating **the applied power of positive thinking,**

CHAPTER 10

Problems vs. Issue Recognition; - Issues vs. Problem Recognition

In the many years of experience as a Pastor, Pastoral Counselor, and Psychotherapist, I have been educated to learn that a majority of folks face circumstances and situations which they are not familiar with, and unfortunately often do not have a solution, or alternative, solutions to what can be referred to as *life adversity*. Some refer to their circumstances and situations as problematic; "a problem." Others refer to their circumstances and or situations as an "issue."

It is important to define and explain the difference:

A Problem: In the broadest sense too often invites the thought of being beyond a reasonable resolution; unsolvable and without a doable, workable solution.

Webster's dictionary defines problem as: *"A matter difficult of solution; difficult to manage; a puzzle or dilemma; a difficult matter requiring solutions."*

Problems often arise as a result of *negative action* or, *reaction*. For instance: If a probable adverse medical condition is neglected, it can become a very real problem.

For example:

1. Neglected high blood pressure can realistically cause a heart attack or stroke and can result in death
2. Neglected high levels of elevated blood sugar can cause kidney failure, diabetic coma, and death
3. A neglected congestive heart failure condition can cause a massive heart attack and death
4. Failure to follow-up on a spot on the lung which shows up in an X-ray can result in lung cancer and death

The obvious negative action, to any of these physical health examples is *lack of action*, or more accurately, *reaction* to a given set of circumstances or situations.

When there is disharmony and discourse in the marital realm __ if neglected__ can result in divorce.

An unresolved "run in" with the boss can, at least, result in being passed over for on the job promotion, and at worst, termination from employment.

Disharmony at the church can cause individuals to become disgruntled __ mad at God and others.__ and drop out of church life in an attempt to disrupt, harm and hurt others, but in fact, hurting the disgruntled church member more than anyone else.

The point is, an unresolved problem confronting an individual's life, can realistically produce a seemingly irresolvable issue, or as Webster's dictionary puts it: *"A difficult matter requiring settlement."*

Thus, as previously stated, a problem or issue in an individual's life is often caused by their direct, or indirect action, (or lack of action) resulting in a reactive negative attitude by others toward the individual, with unknown consequences which all too often are also negative.

Subsequently, without proper application of wisdom, tact, and skillful diplomacy, a problem can become an unresolved issue without a resolution to the harm of all concerned with no positive effect; no positive outcome.

Webster defines an issue as: *"To come or flow forth; to originate from a source; the act of flowing out; that which issues; a decision or result."*

There are multiple definitions, but for our purpose let's combine and focus on two of those definitions. They are: *"To originate from a source;"* and *"a decision or result."*

In summary, both problems and issues are to be dealt with as challenges; challenges are to be met and overcome. To bring about a desired end result, a positive attitude needs to be adopted. The formula: ***the applied power of positive thinking.***

Vignette:

Dennis was an excellent worker; however, he had great difficulty getting to places on time. This had been a pattern throughout his life. He had been late to his Bar Mitzvah; late to his high school graduation; and late to his wedding. He jokingly said he would be late to his own funeral.

He had recently joined a major company as a mechanical drawing engineer. At first, in the beginning his supervisor had overlooked his daily tardiness of 5 or 10 minutes, but as the tardy time frame lengthened he found it necessary to talk to Dennis.

Dennis took the disciplinary warning very well, promised he would "do *better at getting to work on time,*" and for a while was able to do so. Unfortunately, before long he had fallen back into the habit of not being on time. Subsequently, the supervisor again talked to him and warned that such continued behavior could result in termination. Embarrassed, Dennis apologized, stated "*it will not happen again,*" and seriously promised himself that he was going to alter his perpetual habit of being late in arriving for work.

Dennis set his clock one hour ahead, set the alarm one-half hour earlier, and vowed to be an early arriver at his work place. Through determination, he not only achieved his goal of being an early arriver, he became a role model by setting an example for being on-time for all the other employees in his department.

His exemplary action won him much recognition i.e. Employee of the Month, an Outstanding Achievement Award plus, Most Influential Employee, and others.

This account of how Dennis determined to overcome his abhorrent behavior __ through change in attitude and determination __ clearly focuses on the benefits that can be achieved by facilitating *the power of applied positive thinking.*

CHAPTER 11

Knowing When to Say No

When Ronald Regan was president, his wife Nancy sponsored and launched a free from drugs philosophy for young people to resist drugs. The campaign was designed to free young people from street drugs with the slogan, *"Just Say No!"*

The jury is still out on the verdict as to whether or not the program was successful. Be that as it may, the thinking was then, and is now, that the will power and guts to *"Just Say No!"* as opposed to participating and experimenting with drugs by saying *"Yes,"* is measurable.

Unfortunately, too often, the path of least resistance kicks in when young people are faced with tough decisions. It appears as if it is easier to say *"Yes"* than *"No,"* to the enticement of drugs and the temptation decisions for drug experimentation, and eventual drug addiction.

It would seem, by comparison and contrast, decision making usually determines either positive or negative action. Subsequently, negative decisions usually dictates negative action and conversely, positive decisions dictate positive action.

Does this sound like *gibberish*? Perhaps, but it reinforces the axiom of *"truth is stranger than fiction."*

Interestingly, the word *"no"* is a powerful word and has compelling force. Psychiatrists have reported that an infant hears the word *"no"* 3,000 times by the time they reach three years of age. Yet with adulthood and maturity it appears the word *"no"* is often forgotten. The question is: Why? Why is it so difficult to say no to certain circumstances or situations?

While the yes or no decision is a matter of choice, the choice is often influenced by the least path of resistance. That is; the obvious conclusion: with less resistance it is easier to do evil than good. It is easier with less resistance to make the negative or bad decision, than the positive or good decision. Either way, it is always the culmination of an irrational thought, or irrational action process. Obviously, the facilitation of the power of applied positive thinking is always the best choice.

The mind-set encompassing the power of *the applied positive thinking* will be illustrated in the following Vignettes.

Vignette:

Harry was a dedicate employee. He came early to work and stayed later than others. To the co-workers it appeared that Harry was the boss's "pet." The boss was always spending time at Harry's desk and often would even approach Harry as he ate lunch in the company cafeteria dining room. The co-workers didn't know was the truth of the matter, the reason for Mr. Jerrod (the boss) spending so much time with harry was, Harry was being *used* by the boss.

Wanting to receive good, above average employee evaluations Harry went out of his way to daily perform his job task responsibilities. But, at the same time, he strived to also perform the incredible additional tasks the boss demanded of him. His primary role was a financial officer and his direct responsibility was to prepare a monthly accounting budget, to balance income against paid outs, and to publish the budget report statement without error in a timely manner for profit / loss corporate review.

Harry was a proud man and was very pleased with the financial work he accomplished for his company during the five years he had been in the position. His superiors was also pleased and had consistently given him above average, excellent and outstanding evaluation reviews for four out of the past five years. His immediate supervisor was an ambitious A type person always struggling to move up the corporate ladder chain and was in competition for a vacancy in the upper management hierarchy. Subsequently, Mr. Jerrod would manufacture busy work for Harry to accomplish; work which had been assigned to him. He knew Harry would get the work done efficiently and effectively for which he would receive credit. He connived to impress his superiors by completing his own immediate assignments, and at the same time, turning in the above average work done by Harry; work which had been assigned to him to complete at a future date.

Up to this point Harry had never complained or turned down any additionally assigned tasks given to him by his boss. He had willingly accepted the added work load and had diligently performed the work to completion even at the compromise of running out of regular hours on the job to get his own weekly and monthly duties and responsibilities accomplished. He was becoming more and more frustrated and even felt like quitting, a feeling he had not experienced before.

The final straw came when Mr. Jarred requested Harry to finalize his (the boss's) department payroll because he was scheduled to go out of town on company business.

Finalization of the boss's payroll was clearly the responsibility of Mr. Jarred. It was a weekly requirement that Mr. Jarred had to review and sign off on with regard to employee overtime, salary, and cost-to-perform vs. production. As a supervisor he was charged with a responsibility to maintain an acceptable cost-to-perform ratio.

The end of the month was fast approaching and Harry was feverishly working to bring all figures into a balanced focus. Harry knew he would have to necessarily work overtime hours himself without compensation in order to complete all end of month reports.

Since Mr. Jerrod was going out of town on company business he was attempting to hand off to Harry some of his payroll preparation reports. Harry finally found the courage to stand up to his boss. In a kind and considerate way his conversation left little doubt that he was working beyond his capacity and his discussion laid out perimeters for. He said to Mr. Jerrod, *"I have never complained when you have assigned me additional work, but now I need to speak up. I have multiple reports to complete and balance, prior to the end of the month. So I need to ask you, which do you want me to not do, the end of the month reports, or finalize your departments payroll report?*

Mr. Jerrod faced a dilemma. If he ordered Harry to do *his* work instead of the end of the month reports he would personally be in a world of hurt. If he did that he knew immediately his chance for promotion would be jeopardized. On the other hand, if his own department payroll report was *not* completed the employees in the department would not receive a pay check.

Harry patiently waited, while his boss pondered the dilemma, for his answer as to what Mr. Jerrod's priority for him was. Finally the boss spoke: *"Harry, I'll take care of the other Reports."*

As it turned out, Mr. Jerrod cancelled and postponed his out of town business trip and spent the time needed to complete his department's payroll. Harry later learned Mr. Jerrod's report contained many inaccuracies, costing the company a substantial amount of overtime salary, causing the performance costs to sky rocket for the department. Mr. Jerrod was subsequently demoted from supervisor to foreman and transferred to another department.

The point of this vignette is: Harry ultimately stood up for his rights and, in a favorable way, turned an unfavorable situation around by requesting his boss to prioritize his work assignments in order of importance for completion.

Harry had learned to say *"No."* He facilitated ***the applied power of positive thinking.***

CHAPTER 12

Anger / Resolution: Giving / Receiving Apology & Forgiveness

Forgiveness is a unique dynamic. It has been said by some, *"I'll forgive you, but I'll never forget."* Permit a truism: *One cannot forgive without forgetting.* It is a mental impossibility to forgive an act of abuse, physical or emotional offense, or abusive aggressive behavior from a perpetrator. when the one who is offended cannot, or is *unwilling* to *forgive and* to *forget.*

When one attempts to forgive an abusive or offensive act, *but makes no effort to forget the offense,* then every time the one who is offended sees the offender, they are again reminded of the offensive act. When this happens *the act of forgiveness is invalidated because the act has not been forgotten.* The act of forgiveness moves beyond the emotional and mental capacity to forgive because, it is a mental impossibility when the one who is offended, by an act of abuse behavior, is *unwilling* to *forgive and to forget.*

In the words of one, it is said, *"to err is human; to forgive is divine."* What is the meaning of this profound, powerful statement expression? Simply this: the ability to forgive and forget borders on Providential happenstance and is akin to an act of kindness inspired and motivated by a Higher Power i.e. a Divine source.

In the most actual and realistic sense forgiveness consists of four dynamic elements. Each of which *necessarily must* be applied in order for unconditional forgiveness to be effective and successful. In conducting marriage counseling therapy, for dysfunctional marital relationships, the writer has suggested to numerous couples the following formula for forgiveness; positive results have been observed through application of these suggested principals in bringing about authentic and genuine forgiveness.

In therapy, a therapeutic goal is set, which when reached through application of these suggested dynamics, the parties to the abusive and offensive behavior patterns can learn *to* agree, even if the agreement is to *disagree agreeably*. Progress can then be made toward forgiving, forgetting, and receiving forgiveness.

The formula dynamics, for successful closure and forgiveness, that can be applied for successful closure and forgiveness to any dysfunctional relationship, are set forth as follows:

Anger: John and Gladys had been married for one year before they had what they considered to be a "real" argument. John had increased his beer drinking. At first he had only one or two beers. Then three or four, and then to a six pack every night when he came home from work.

Gladys hated his drinking. She claimed his personality changed when he drank and he became angry and belligerent. The expense of buying beer to support his habit had impacted their tight budget. They could no longer afford to buy the birth-control medication Gladys had come to depend on to keep from getting pregnant. Subsequently, she had been forced to go off the pill and soon became pregnant, and had given birth to little Timothy who was now three-months old.

One evening, John came home from work later than usual. He had stopped to hang-out and have a few rounds with some of the fellows from work. It had been a bad day for Gladys.

Baby Timothy had been fussy; the weather had been hotter than usual and their upstairs apartment had been miserably hot and uncomfortable. The unfavorable combination of things had whetted her anger causing her temper to flame and flare.

John was not prepared for her angry remark of, and subsequent confrontation of, *"you're drunk again!"*

He did not think he was drunk and neither did he know exactly how to react. His temper also flared causing him to say unpleasant things to Gladys which he would later regret.

John struck out at one of Gladys's weakest points and called her a "fat bitch." Gladys was still struggling to lose 20 pounds of "baby fat" she had gained during pregnancy.

John suddenly realized what he had said and was immediately sorry when he saw the hurt look cross Gladys's face. However, he was not sorry enough to apologize at the time.

Gladys's reply to his criticism was also criticism; *"You're no lightweight yourself. Look at your beer gut!"* John flinched at her stinging remark. It was true, he reasoned, he was 20 pounds heavier than when they married. And he was very conscious, of the protruding belly overhanging his belt. He responded in the only way he knew how; with more criticism. *"It takes one to know one!"* he childishly replied.

Over the next few days, John and Gladys kissed and made-up. This dysfunctional behavior and conduct was to become their life-style during the months and years ahead. More harmful and brittle criticism would hurtfully drive them apart, time and time again, in what is known in counseling vocabulary as "the Cycle of Violence."

Simply said the "Cycle of Violence" begins with verbal abuse through angry expressed words and criticism and, escalates eventually erupting into physical abuse and violence, after which it then subsides. The perpetrator begs for and receives momentary forgiveness. In the ensuing "make-up" or "honeymoon" stage all appears to be forgiven, and life has never been sweeter, until the Cycle of Violence" starts all over again.

Synopsis:

There are a number of dynamics that need to be addressed in this Vignette.

First: Anger needs to be dealt with at, or as near as possible, to the time the event causing anger to occur. For example:

Gladys's Anger: In the vignette Gladys had let her anger build to the point of being out of control (this dynamic will be addressed later in this study). As a matter of fact, the emotion experienced by Gladys was fueling the anger. Therefore, the anger needed to only reach the boiling point causing her to explode. That point was reached when John came home late, drunker than usual.

Anger controlled her; John became the target for her.

Secondly, John's Anger:

John responded in surprise; surprise at Gladys's action. He reacted in kind with more increased anger fueled by criticism. It appears as if John's mind-set has become an act of taking Gladys for granted even at this early stage __ less than two years __ into the marriage. Up until now Gladys had stopped nagging John about his drinking. Subsequently, this was a signal to him that she approved . Therefore, John perceived this to mean that Gladys not only approved but gave him her permission.

John's anger reached the boiling point because of his misconception regarding Gladys' approval of his drinking. This is a classic example of miscommunication (which will be discussed later on in this work).

It appears as if Gladys stopped nagging and complaining to John about his drinking, thinking and hoping that John would come to his senses and stop drinking. The exact opposite happened: John had misinterpreted Gladys's lack of complaining and nagging as her finally having accepted and approved of his alcoholic behavior.

Evidenced here is the very act of bringing together two dynamics: miscommunication and misunderstanding that fostered unresolved conflict. Conflict which can only find a solution in resolution through change in conduct, i.e. starting with apology and forgiveness (which will be discussed later on in this study).

Anger is both a *positive* and *negative* force. It is O.K. to be angry. Even the Bible states: *"Be angry, and sin not."* Ephesians 4:26 KJV. Anger needs to be expressed in order to "vent' one's emotional feelings. Anger can be good or destructive. To be a good dynamic anger needs to be good, constructive, and positive; anger must be controlled.

As previously stated, anger needs to be expressed at the time of, or as close as possible to the time of the event or circumstance, initiating the anger.

This concept is so basic that it is often overlooked by those who are angered, thus, preventing a workable solution. The anger control factor is of paramount importance in order to initiate a successful resolution.

Suffice it to say that:

1. Anger must be controlled
2. Anger must be expressed (at, or as close to the time of, the event causing anger as possible)

Bottled Anger: If anger is not expressed it is turned inside, internalized, suppressed and begins to build up internally. Each time anger is suppressed it build up more and more and becomes "aged anger." Persistence in continuing to let unexpressed anger build up on top of aged anger produces bitterness toward the one to whom the anger is directed.

The "key" to successful resolution, in the clinical therapeutic relationship, is to guide the client or patient to face the here and now and to stay in touch with reality.

There is very little, if anything, that can be done about past events which have caused disputes, in a situation involving marriage, friendships, or any other type relationship.

Conversely, there is very little, if anything, that can be done to affect the future of a disputed relationship, unless and until focus is placed on the here and now, that is *"right now; today."*

Subsequently, for two persons to work through a dispute to successful resolution there are key ingredients that need to be discussed.

The first ingredient: There must be a sincere desire by the involved parties; obviously, desire in and of itself, will not bring resolution.

The second ingredient: There must be motivation; when there is sincere desire to bring about resolution that desire initiates motivation. However, desire and motivation combined will not bring forth a successful resolution. There is a third dynamic ingredient.

The third ingredient: Application; put them all together they spell "successful resolution."

Here is the Formula: DMA

DESIRE = D

MOTIVATION = M

APPLICATION = A

There other dynamics involved in dealing with anger. We have already quoted the Scripture; as a matter of fact, this quote, *"Be angry and sin not..."* Ephesians 4:26 KJV, gives a person permission to be angry with a caution, that is, *"...sin not."*

Elsewhere in Scripture another piece of sage advice is offered: *"Don't let the sun go down on your wrath..."* Ephesians 4:26 KJV.

So from this, we can understand that a certain amount of "controlled" anger is O.K. It is only when anger goes out of control that it becomes "bad anger."

"Bad Anger" can be described and defined as, when a person *"flies off the handle"* and goes out of control, flaming and flaring, exhibiting a low boiling point with a short fuse resulting in angry inflammable words being said, which have not been thoroughly thought through.

Unfortunately, harmful and hurtful words can never be taken back or recalled. They leave a lasting and indelible impression on the mind of the person to whom they are directed.

Since those words are indelible how then, can the offended person ever work though them, by forgiving the offender, in order to retain or maintain a friendship, or relationship with the offender? That is an excellent question, and brings us to the "other dynamics" involved in dealing with anger.

Anger, *necessarily,* has to be resolved *through* forgiveness.

As previously discussed, forgiveness is a unique dynamic. Permit a repetitious statement: It has been said by some, *"I will forgive, but I will never forget."* Permit a bold but true statement: One cannot forgive without forgiving. It is a mental impossibility, to forgive an act of abuse, physical or emotional offensive or abusive aggression from a perpetrator, when the one who is offended cannot, or is unwilling to *forgive and forget.*

When one attempts to forgive an offensive act __ but makes no effort to forget the offense __ then each time the one who has forgiven sees the offender they are again reminded of the offensive act.

The act of forgiveness has to move beyond the emotional and mental human capacity. In the words of one, it is said: *"To err is human; to forgive is divine."*

What is meant by this profound expression? Simply this:

To forgive and forget borders on a providential happenstance akin to actiom inspired by a Higher Power.

Forgiveness consists of four dynamic active elements which must necessarily be applied in order for *complete forgiveness* to be effective and successful.

As a psychotherapist the writer has suggested to numerous couples in marriage therapy the following formula to apply in order to obtain complete and final forgiveness. When applied the formula helped them to resolve issues and adopt these principles to bring about successful forgiveness.

It needs to be stated that, when a therapeutic goal has been reached wherein the involved parties to the abusive and offensive behavior patterns can agree, to disagree agreeably, progress can be made toward forgiving and obtaining forgiveness.

Those dynamics which were shared and suggested are presented herewith:

Apology: Apology is essential and absolutely necessary for the offender to apologize with a sincere apology and ask for forgiveness from the offended. This set in motion a **4 step process.**

For example, in the opening Vignette (under anger) both Gladys and John were, at least, verbally abusive to each other. In order for them to be able to face the here-and-now both needed to claim ownership and responsibility for their irresponsible and dysfunctional conduct and behavior.

For instance, John could have started the **4 step process** by apologizing to Gladys for his unacceptable behavior, thus:

John: *Gladys, I really do love you. I know I don't always show it by my actions and I admit that I have been abusive to you by my actions. I want to apologize to you from the bottom of my heart; I want to be a better husband. Will you accept my apology?*

Gladys: *Yes, John, you have been verbally abusive and disrespectful of me as your wife. If you are sincere, and really mean it, I will accept your apology.*

John: *I am very sincere in my apology. I know I have hurt you with my actions and I don't want to hurt you anymore. You are my wife and I love you; you are the mother of our child and that will never change. I want to be the best husband I know how to be. Will you help me to become a better husband and father?*

Gladys: *I believe you are sincere John. I will accept your apology and help you.*

John: *Thank you for accepting my apology and offering to help me become a better husband, father, and parent. I will work hard to become the best me, I know how to be.*

This accomplishes the apology process; 50% of the work has been done. Now comes the other 50%; forgiveness.

Forgiveness:

John: *Thank you Gladys for accepting my apology. I now want to ask for your forgiveness. I know that I have been disrespectful, rude and unloving toward you Gladys. I want to change. I want to be the best husband, and father I can be. With your help I can. Will you forgive me Gladys?*

Gladys: *You really sound sincere John. I trust you. I think you do want to change. I am going to take your request for forgiveness seriously; I will forgive you, John.*

Gladys: *John, I also need to offer an apology to you. John, will you accept my apology for my behavior and conduct?*

John: *Yes. Gladys, I accept your apology*

Gladys: *Like you, John, I also need to ask for your forgiveness; will you forgive me?*

John: *Yes. I will; I will forgive you, Gladys.*

The couple could seal the new covenant with a hug and a kiss.

This 4 step Apology and Forgiveness process clears the air, and cleans the slate, for a new start in their existing marital relationship. It represents an emptying of the minds with regard to the disruptive relationship.

The empty slate (chalkboard / whiteboard) signifies and symbolically represents, that the unacceptable behavior and conduct has been erased; forgiven and forgotten.

To summarize, **the 4 step process**: Apology and Forgiveness can become *a positive healing force* when applied to dysfunctional relationships, such as: "*he said; she said*" blaming, or "Cycle of Violence" circumstance..

The Higher Power__ Creator of the Universe__ wanted life for His creation to be *humble* and *simplistic*.

Man has chosen a different path, complicating life, causing great distance to separate man not only from His Creator, but also from his fellowman, and specifically from his life-partner and soul mate; his spouse.

If there ever was a time for mankind to seek peace-of-mind, through use of sound value-judgment, it is *now*, in our complex, negative, and turbulent society.

The author contends that man can only achieve peace-of mind by ***facilitating the applied power of positive thinking.***

CHAPTER 13

Isolation – Self-imposed / From Others

Isolation is a defense mechanism. When an individual experiences a severe loss or a traumatic happening in their life several dynamics surface and come into focus.

One of those dynamics is classified as Post Traumatic Stress Disorder PTST. In psychological terminology the major symptoms are the repetitious reoccurring of a traumatic event __ in the mind of the one affected by the event __ and the re-living of that severe and emotional experience.

Up until recently this condition was almost always connected to armed service veterans returning from war that had been exposed to traumatic battle-field combat experiences and was diagnosed as Post Traumatic Stress Disorder, also referred to as PTST.

More recently, this diagnosis has become more commonly used in the psychological venue by psychiatrists and psychologists to describe symptoms affecting patients in the everyday life cycle who have been exposed to traumatic events and are having reoccurring "flash-backs" to that specific event.

Persons experiencing this, or other symptoms resulting from trauma, often want to be "left-alone" and thus isolate themselves from others as a defense mechanism; realistically, isolation is very real a form of "self-punishment used as an "escape" mechanism.

It doesn't have to be that way. If an individual receives counseling or psychotherapy they can be encouraged to reach out to others and, the isolation factor will be defused.

When an individual is a willing participant in constructive counseling either by a professional counselor or a qualified, concerned family member the end result can be very positive and productive.

It has been said, *"talk is cheap,"* however, it can be one of the most valuable tools in the arsenal of a qualified therapist interacting with a client, and can be instrumental in helping an isolated individual move forward through the isolation, when they successfully facilitate ***the applied power of positive thinking.***

Vignette:

After an extended illness Susan's father passed away from a terminal disease of colon cancer. As the primary care giver Susan was devastated.__ even though her father's passing was an expected death. Two years before she had lost her mother in an automobile accident; the loss of both parents was overwhelming.

An only child she had been very close to both parents. Because of her father's terminal diagnosis, and subsequent rapid decline, Susan felt obligated to assume the role of primary care giver for her father while he was a hospice patient. Therefore, she never had adequate time to appropriately grieve the loss of her mother and work through her bereavement, grief and sadness before her father passed.

As she struggled with the loss of her father the "bottled" grief for her mother came flooding back and combined with the un-expressed grief over the loss of her mother. Feelings of helplessness and hopelessness appeared to consume her. She was in a quandary; she didn't know where, or to whom to turn.

A ray of sunshine broke through the cloud of hopelessness when the hospice bereavement counselor reached out to her. Through on-going contact the bereavement counselor encouraged Susan to enroll in a bereavement program sponsored by the hospice agency. At first she hesitated about joining feeling others would observe her crying and, venting her bereavement and grief and, she believed they would not understand and embarrass her.

The bereavement counselor continued encouraging her to join the bereavement program sessions. Finally, abandoning her thought of embarrassment, she was determined to participate and share her own grief and the grief of others who had also experienced losses.

Six months after attending bereavement group sessions Susan had an epiphany and was able to laugh again. To focus her mind in another direction she enrolled in a community college self-help class.

Slowly but surely Susan began to take charge of her life again and to stay in control. She vowed to herself that she would never lose sight of the love and compassion she had experienced with her mother and father. Ultimately she came to realize she must move her life past the pool of pain she had been walking in, and come out on the other side.

She had been so impressed with the hospice program __ which managed her father's care __ that she decided to become a volunteer in the program, with the thought of touching lives and bringing a ray of sunshine into the life of others who were living with a life-limiting, terminal illness.

Ten years later Susan is still a volunteer in a hospice program agency. This is a clear cut example of what *can* be accomplished through desire, motivation, and action *(DMA) when the *applied* power of positive thinking is used.

*(DMA) discussed elsewhere in this publication

CHAPTER 14

Value Judgment;
Application Of

Decision making is one of the most important actions an individual can ever make.

A decision to follow the conscienous, or to "mask" the conscienous and follow a pattern of delusional behavior, often camouflages the reality of truth. Subsequently, the ability to make a sound decision __ to do the right thing __ is influenced by an individual's sense of values; the ability to use value judgment.

When an individual has no sense of value judgment they are easily influenced by negativism. Therefore, sound decision making is obscured by cloudy thinking, which lowers resistance levels, often resulting in criminal activity.

The value of choosing between "right" and "wrong" is diminished and persons, who would not normally be prone to crime, now view committing crimes such as robbery, home invasions, rape, burglary, up to and including murder, with little, or no remorse.

Poet laureate Robert Burns (1786) wrote in an "*Ode To A Mouse,*" "*The best laid plans of mice and men, often go astray.*" The obvious conclusion is, that regardless of how well one plans, circumstances may not always work out according to plan.

Therefore, one can hope, want, and plan, to do the right thing, but unless and until effort is applied to positively move the plan forward, the plan, in and of itself, will fail.

Subsequently, plans should always be for the best outcome, however, reality dictates one should always be prepared, to accept the worst; plan for the best, prepare for the worst.

Vignette:

Jamie Ryan never liked her name. She liked it even less when she learned that after she and her two sisters were born her mother and father decided to try once more for a son. Prior to learning their next child would also be a girl they had picked out the name James, to honor the grandfather on their father's side. With the birth of another girl her parents had shortened the names James to Jamie. Jamie was 13 years old before she learned the truth about how she had received her name.

Upon learning how she had received the name she despised she became angrier and angrier at her parents and rebelled. She began running with the wrong crowd, started breaking her parent's curfew and stayed out past mid-night even on school nights. The more her parents disciplined her, the angrier Jamie become; her anger drove her to start experimenting with marijuana. She was arrested in a high school party drug bust along with several of her school friends.

Released into the custody of her parents she was grounded, with the condition that the grounding would be lifted when her behavior improved. Jamie was furious; she began to cut classes with a male school friend. Her belligerence resulted in a pregnancy. When she shared the news of pregnancy with the boy-friend he encouraged her to get an abortion which he promised to pay for; he refused to marry her.

Jamie faced a dilemma causing her great anxiety, frustration, and stress. She pondered what to do: tell her parents; get an abortion, or give birth to the baby and adopt it out.

These were legitimate and profound questions facing Jamie, with no apparent or obvious solution. She kept asking herself: *"What should I do?* And *what would her fate be?* She recognized time was her enemy; she would soon necessarily have to make a decision.

Jamie confided in Physical Education teacher who referred her to the school nurse and psychologist. Each supported her with active listening, heard her story, and refused to give her advice. Rather, both emphasized the fact that even at age 13 she was a young adult, and each suggested that she consider all of the alternatives available to her, including telling her parents, __ which Jamie already knew __ and to make her own personal decision.

Jamie was now more confused than ever. Contrary to the school nurse and psychologist's suggestion Jamie had already considered all of the options. In her heart, she knew she had to take drastic measures; she knew she had to tell her parents. She feared the confrontation. She also knew the baby's father didn't want her, or the baby. She also knew that she could not have an abortion. She had long been taught that abortion was murder.

She had underestimated the love and understanding of her parents. They listened carefully without interruption as she tearfully poured out her heart about her dilemma. They comforted her with compassion and kind heartedness. After hearing her story the parents simply asked her if she knew what all of the alternatives were. She told them she did. The parents counseling session ended with the parents assuring Jamie that they would support her in whatever decision she made.

Jamie continued to ponder her life-changing situation for the next week and then announced to her parents that she had decided to continue her pregnancy and give birth to the baby. The decision was welcomed by her parents and family.

Postscript: Jamie continued as a student during her pregnancy, finished the school year, and gave birth to a 6 pound 8 ounce healthy baby boy. To honor her parents and grandparents she named the baby James.

Finally, although not a sibling off-spring, her parents had a boy in the family; a grandson named James.

Author's comment:
This vignette is a touching and profound example of a teen-age individual, doing the right thing by using sound value judgment, combined with *the applied power of positive thinking.*

CHAPTER 15

Change: Past, Present, Future

Past

Someone has said, *"You can't walk backwards through the future."*

The implication is that, in order to move forward in a positive and constructive direction one has to focus with eyes wide open on forward movement.

This would appear to be over-lapping with "Goal Setting" as discussed in chapter 6.

At the risk of being repetitious and redundant the consistency would, in fact, fall within the dynamics of realistic, doable, and reachable Goal Setting, i.e.

1. Short Term goal
2. Intermediate Goal
3. Long Term goals (Refer to Chapter 6)

These concepts would adequately and succinctly put in place *the applied power of positive thinking*, with regard to the future and, at the same time, introduce and encompass the past.

Obviously, if an individual stays focused on the past, i.e. *"shoulda, coulda, woulda"* outcome attitude, the thinking becomes cloudy and is lost in the fog of reverie.

Conclusion: The employment of *the applied power of positive thinking* would dictate forward focus and movement for credible, positive achievement.

It needs to be recognized that, failed circumstances can be used as learning tools, providing stepping stones for gainful learning experience, so that one does not apply non-productive actions in the future.

Recognition surges to the forefront, bringing acutely into focus the fact that, the past is just that; the past. It cannot be recalled to live over again; it is history.

Summary: While past experiences can point up non-productive actions or failures, they become invaluable lessons for bringing about credible, viable achievement; that is, in the here and now, and into the future.

Vignette:

Cite Abraham Lincoln's failures and achievements.

Abraham Lincoln is reputed to be one of the great __ if not the greatest __ presidents of the United States.

Be that as it may be, he had his share of failures along with his successes.

Both his failures and successes are briefly listed in the time frame that follows:

FAILURES	SUCCESSES	DATE
Lost his Job and was Defeated as a Candidate for State Legislature	Elected Captain of the Illinois Militia of the Black Hawk War	1832
Business Failure	Appointed Postmaster New Salem, Illinois; also appointed Deputy in Sangamon County	1833
	Elected to Illinois State Legislature	1834
Fiancé Passes Away		1835
Sustained Nervous Breakdown	Re-elected to Illinois State Legislature Licensed to Practice Law in Illinois Courts	1836
	Instrumental in Moving Illinois State Capital from Vandalia to Springfield; Joined John T. Stewart as Law Partner	1837

Defeated for Speaker	Nominated by Whig Party Caucus for Illinois House Speaker Re-elected to Illinois House; Served as Which Floor Leader	1838
	Chosen as Presidential elector by Whig Part Convention; Admitted to Practice Law in U.S Circuit Court	1839
	First case argued before Illinois Supreme Legislature	1840
	Partnered with Stephen T. Logan in New Law Practice	1841
	Admitted to practice law in U.S. District Court	1842
Defeated for nomination to Congress		1843
	Established Private Law Practice with William H, Herndon as a Junior Partner	1844
	Elected to Congress	1846
Lost his Re-nomination	Chose not to run for Congress, per rule Of rotation Among Which Party	1848

Rejected for land officer	Admitted to Practice Law in U.S Supreme Court; Declined Appointment as Secretary And Governor of Oregon Territory	1849
Defeated for U.S Senate	Elected to Illinois State Legislature; Declined Seat to run for U.S Senate	1854
Defeated for Nomination for Vice President		1856
Defeated Again in run for U.S Senate		1858
	Elected President Of The United States	1860

There are various common theories on the origin of the nickname "Honest Abe." One story relates that, when Abraham Lincoln was working as a clerk in a store in New Salem, he once took 6 1/4 cents too much from a customer. That night when the store closed, he walked three miles to return the woman's money.

A story goes that, another time a customer who had asked for 1/2 pound of tea was mistakenly given only 1/4 pound because Lincoln had absent-mindedly left a 1/4 weight on the scales. The story relates, very early in the morning, when Lincoln discovered the mistake, he walked a long way to give the customer the right amount of tea.

Other Lincoln nicknames included "The Rail Splitter;" "The Great Emancipator;" and "Father Abraham."

"The Great Emancipator" refers to Lincoln's issuance of the Emancipation Proclamation and his strong support of the Thirteenth Amendment which ended slavery in the United States.

"Father Abraham" refers to Lincoln's leadership during the Civil War and his goal of ending slavery.

These two Vignettes solidly prove that, when you have a realistic, reasonable, and doable plan the next to impossible can be accomplished by facilitating ***the applied power of positive thinking.***

Present

We hear a lot today about change. As a matter of fact, Barack Obama ran a successful campaign for president of the United States __ and won __ in 2008 on the slogan of ***"Yes, You Can," and "Change You Can Believe In."***

There is no credible or conclusive argument that change *cannot* be a viable and positive force in the life of an individual, group, or society at large. However, "change" *just for the sake of change* is not necessarily always good, or positive.

Unfortunately, too many people believe in that old cliché of *"You can't teach an old dog new tricks,"* and conclude that this cliché is applicable to many or all situations.

The truth of the matter is, while many clichés and old wives tales hold some grains of truth for certain situations today. Change is not one of those situations and this chapter will demonstrate and illustrate with a Vignette that the old cliché *"You can't teach an old dog new tricks,"* **is false!** The old cliché flies in the face of those who have, in fact, even at advanced age been successful beyond expectation.

Any person regardless of age, color, ethnicity, or religious preference needs to recognize and admit that choice necessarily must begin to initiate the mind of the individual. There are several dynamics which have to be taken into serious consideration with regard to making a sound decision. These dynamics are:

1. Recognizing the need *for* change
2. Desire for change to affect the better
3. Willingness *to* change
4. Instigating the "how to" change
5. Developing a plan and method *for* change
6. Applying the method by setting the plan in motion

Each of these dynamics will be briefly discussed:

1. Recognizing the need for change

There is an old expression which states, *"If it isn't broken, don't try to fix it."* The obvious thought being, if a method, procedure, or principle is working sufficiently avoid trying to improve upon it, re-design it, or "fix it."

To substantiate and support that thinking there is axiom, i.e. *"Don't try to re-invent the wheel."* The implied thought is, *"How many ways can you improve on a wheel?"* The wheel is round, it rolls, and it consistently runs in a continuum in either forward or reverse movement.

Therefore, *how do* you improve on, or re-invent a wheel?

On the other hand, if change is used *simply for the sake of change* without any positive effect, then it would appear to be an exercise in futility with no apparent or obvious end result.

2. Desire for change to affect the better

When desire for change is motivated by action to effect betterment the action is credible and responsible and often positive in bringing about the successful end result thus, positive change.

3. Willingness *to* change

In order to have change with positive results, either individually or in a group setting, there needs to be a strong majority desire motivated by a collaborative consensus among the players who will influence, or put more simply, bring about positive change.

4. Instigating the "how to" change

So far we have discussed recognizing a need *for* change; the Desire for Change to affect the better; the Willingness *to* change and, now we will briefly discuss instigating the "how to" affect a change.

In order to facilitate Instigating the "how to" affect a change all of the foregoing dynamics have to necessarily be definitively in focus. Otherwise, for an individual, a company, government, or society at large the concept for change slides out of focus and ends up as cloudy intellect or wishful thinking.

Instigating a change starts with a solid and sound idea for improvement brought about through positive change. The concept and principle is the same for an individual, a group, a government, country or society in general. The envisioned or intended change must be possible, doable, and economically feasible geared toward achieving a positive end result.

5. Developing a plan and method *for* change

Good intentions about wanting to do something good is not a credible and viable reason for change. Therefore, in order to effectively bring about change a reliable and sound plan needs to be put in place.

There is an axiom which states, *"Develop a plan; follow the plan."* The obvious conclusion is to develop a plan, and put it in place before attempting to achieve a given goal.

The plan has to be realistic, doable, and workable to implement change. The plan necessarily must be developed around a credible and viable strategy, which will propel steps to a realistic implementation ultimately leading to a desired, effective, positive end result.

Otherwise the poet laureate Robert Burns *"Ode To A Mouse,"* i.e. *"The best laid plans of mice and men often go astray"* pre-determines the result. By contrast and comparison; if the plan is not realistic, doable, workable, and feasible, the plan will *"go astray."*

6. Applying the method by setting the plan in motion

Applying the plan for change with a credible, viable method.

Once a constructive plan has been formulated, and a method of application chosen, the plan of action can be put in motion to move forward. By applying the foregoing dynamics the possibility for obtaining any realistic change goal can be accomplished.

Spiritual persons and followers of Christ's teaching have an axiom plan: *"Just one life, 'twill soon be past; only what's done for Christ will last."*

For the believer this axiom plan appropriately captures their faith and belief in their leader; Christ, presenting very explicit and definitive assurance for the Christian belief system. Their philosophy is in their faith; it obviously does not leave any room for failure. In their mind their belief system is *"fail safe."*

By contrast and parallel __ for society at large __ the present is the here and now 7 days a week, 24 hours a day, 365 days a year. When a 24 hour period has elapsed the day is over. It fades into dusk, and the dawning of another 24 hour period begins. Long story short: yesterday is history, tomorrow is future, when it gets here it will be today; today is all that we have. While we tentatively plan for the future, an individual's plan must necessarily include and focus on today.

Realistically, whatever an individual accomplishes, or whatever an individual's actions achieve during the waking hours, out of the 24 hour time frame __ usually 15 to 18 hours, depending on the individual's sleep pattern __ determines the level of positive or negative achievement for any individual's specific plan.

The attitude and mind set an individual chooses determines the level of achievement; the choice has to be individual and personal. Obviously attitude can be, and is, responsible for causing unintended results and determines whether or not an individual want to be, or to become, a positive achiever in obtaining a given plan.

Once a plan has been made, and decision reached on how to put that plan in motion, the level of credible achievement and accomplishment is determined by desire, which rules motivation. Thus, we are once again influenced by Desire, Motivation, and Action (DMA), and a Positive Mental Attitude (PMA) discussed in Chapter 7 of this work.

Without thinking through what has been previously presented the presentation may sound like "psycho babble" or "gobley gook."

In order to clarify what has been discussed the writer has carefully chosen a powerful Vignettes and is published here to aptly demonstrate the *applied* power of positive thinking

This powerful vignette is presented to demonstrate beyond a reasonable doubt how the importance of formulating a plan is and, with a passionate determination how, to tenaciously cling to the pursuit of the plan, to successfully obtain fulfillment of the plan.

Vignette

In 2009 a remarkable story appeared in the *Greely Tribune* news about an elderly *man who, for 65 years, had successfully pursued his plan and ultimately received his high school diploma at 84 years of age.

From the graduates account the story read in part, *"...I was 18 when I was drafted out of school during WW II...and sent to Japan"*... he relates, *"after the war ended me and my fiancé were married and I brought my new bride back to the United States,"* where he went back to farming.

Through persistence and dogged determination he diligently pursued and obtained the high school diploma.

Long story short, the military veteran pursued his high school diploma and eventually obtained fulfillment of his plan and dream.

At the presentation, one of his first humorous verbal reactions was, *"...I'm 84 years old now; what am I going do with a diploma? Look for a job?"*

A graduation celebration was arranged by family and friends with cake and ice cream. After graduation, the new graduate said, *"I thank everybody from the bottom of my heart."* He went on to say, *"This is more than I would have gotten if I had graduated in the 40's."*

This is a touching and true story. The obvious conclusion: Perseverance, linked with dogged determination was the catalyst responsible for fulfilling this individual's plan and ultimate lifelong goal; the combined dynamics of perseverance, and dogged determination validated the success factor formula, that is, ***the applied power of positive thinking.***

*Name withheld for confidentiality

Vignette

The headline in the Komonews dated July 26, 2009, read: **"Oldest in His Class, First in His Family to Graduate."**

The new *graduate left high school in the 9th grade and joined the navy. He later earned his high school equivalency diploma. When he retired from the Navy in 1999 he decided that it was *"now or never"* for him to pursue a college degree. His plan came to fruition when he enrolled at the University of Washington, Tacoma.

The story line in the Komonews read, in part, *"It is hard to pick out a face in the crowd at a graduation; there are so many students at the University of Washington, Tacoma 2007 graduating class.*

"But one student stands out... maybe it's his age... of 78 years." *"A guy who..."* compared to other students, *"...is their grandparent's age, taking classes with them."*

During the long drive from Bremerton to Tacoma for four years was stressful and often discouraging and, he *"...had his doubts..."* that he would finish and, was tempted to turn back. But, even though he stuck out from other student, he renewed his determination and reasoned, *"... they look at me like the old man and the sea, wondering 'what the heck is he doing here?'*

If they would have asked him, he would have answered, *"...what I am doing is living a lifelong dream-getting that college degree I always wanted."*

His family and friends would have simply said, *"That's the kind of guy he is."*

The new college graduate is living proof that you are never too old to formulate a plan and achieve a lifelong dream.

At 78 years of age he is the first in his family to graduate from college.

His humble responses: *"I did it. I did it finally."*

This Vignette appropriately demonstrates and illustrates the importance of formulating a plan, and the absolute necessity for a making a positive decision to facilitate **the applied power of positive thinking.**

*Name withheld for confidentiality

Future

Despite those who claim to believe in astrology, fortune telling, or are clairvoyant, literally, no one can accurately or credibly look into the future. If this was possible there would be multiple millionaires made by the lottery, the casinos would be out of business and, there would probably be a successful third political party.

Looking into and, predicting the future is realistically impossible; it simply cannot be done.

While it is realistically *impossible* to forecast, or predict the future, it is realistically *possible* to mold the future.

How does one do that? As has been stated, successful achievement and accomplishments begins with an attitude fostered and nurtured by desire. The Desire, Motivation, and Application discussed in Chapter 7 as DMA. The desire is formed by attitude which in turn is moved forward by motivation culminating in successful achievement.

Within reason, nothing is really impossible to achieve for a motivated individual through the facilitation of *the applied power of positive thinking.*

Vignette

The headline in the Komonews dated July 26, 2009, read: **"Oldest in His Class, First in His Family to Graduate."**

The new *graduate left high school in the 9th grade and joined the navy. He later earned his high school equivalency diploma. When he retired from the Navy in 1999 he decided that it was *"now or never"* for him to pursue a college degree. His plan came to fruition when he enrolled at the University of Washington, Tacoma.

The story line in the Komonews read, in part, *"It is hard to pick out a face in the crowd at a graduation; there are so many students at the University of Washington, Tacoma 2007 graduating class.*

"But one student stands out… maybe it's his age… of 78 years." "A guy who…" compared to other students, *"…is their grandparent's age, taking classes with them."*

During the long drive from Bremerton to Tacoma for four years was stressful and often discouraging and, he *"…had his doubts…"* that he would finish and, was tempted to turn back. But, even though he stuck out from other students, he renewed his determination and reasoned, *"…they look at me like the old man and the sea, wondering 'what the heck is he doing here?'*

If they would have asked him, he would have answered, *"…what I am doing is living a lifelong dream-getting that college degree I always wanted."*

His family and friends would have simply said, *"That's the kind of guy he is."*

The new college graduate is living proof that you are never too old to formulate a plan, work the plan, and achieve a lifelong dream.

At 78 years old he is the first in his family to graduate from college. His humble responses: *"I did it. I did it finally."*

This Vignette appropriately demonstrates and illustrates the importance of formulating a plan and, the absolute necessity for making a positive decision __ to successfully obtain a positive end result __ by facilitating ***the applied power of positive thinking***.

*Name withheld for confidentiality

CHAPTER 16

Endurance

There is alleged to be a Biblical quote which states: *"...this too, shall pass."* However, it is believed to have come from the Sufis; Muslim Mystics.

This is a truism in reality; all things *do* come to an end. Unfortunately all too often an individual does not have control over what kind of end that will be.

Those who do have control do not always take control. For example those who engage in criminal activity often end up behind bars; that is *their "end."* Not a happy ending for those who are arrested, charged with a crime and, are convicted.

But it *was their choice*; there are those individual who are willing to violate the laws of the land, knowing full well the consequences and penalty when apprehended, arrested, convicted and incarcerated.

Unfortunately, the punishment does not always match the crime committed. In other words, the punishment does not fit the crime.

This is an extreme example for negative endurance. Let's consider two examples of positive endurance ending with successful results, illustrated with short stories called Vignettes.

Vignette No.1:

A colleague, psychotherapist and friend, was experiencing painful ill health. The condition exacerbated causing severe pain; he checked himself into an Emergency Room at a local hospital for examination. He was subsequently admitted as an outpatient. Tests were performed and he was diagnosed with urine retention; closer observation revealed he needed dialysis.

The primary physician informed him that the dialysis session could possibly be *"a onetime procedure"* which could jump-start his kidneys to start functioning. He later told me, *"This was the plan."*

As it turned out, the subsequent diagnosis was *"renal failure;"* a condition which necessitated dialysis 3 X's a week.

This diagnosis would have been devastating for the average person, but for my psychologist friend, who had a medical background __ and was also a clergy person __ he appeared to be taking it in stride.

Within a week he was discharged from the hospital and began a lifelong regime of dialysis. It became a necessity for him to change his diet and eating habits to healthier foods. He appeared to adapt to the dialysis routine and to maintain a myriad number of medications he was taking for diabetes, high blood pressure, etc.

At this writing __ 7 years later, still on dialysis __ he is now performing his own dialysis at home and says he is *"coping appropriately, as well as can be expected."*

Although the endurance of my psychologist colleague will ultimately end in death, he is a prime example of someone who did, and will __ *unlike many who would have refused dialysis and would have simply given up* __ continue to experience a near normal life, for the rest of his life, as a dialysis patient.

My doctor friend chose a viable and credible alternative, by facilitating **the applied power of positive thinking.**

Vignette No. 2:

Another example of positive endurance involves another colleague and friend, a *medical doctor. My colleague had been diagnosed with prostate cancer. A robotic prostatectomy was performed after which, he survived three years living with one of the slowest growth types of cancer.

At the time of our initial meeting his vision had dimmed causing legal blindness. His faith in an orthodox belief system and, his own strong personal faith in a higher power appeared to sustain him.

Each time I visited he was alert and presented with a pleasant affect and up attitude. I drew personal inspiration from our interventions. While my visits were intended to bring a ray of sunshine to his life, I always seemed to come away, with a larger ray than I would bring.

The doctor had experienced a very successful career and practice as a general practitioner for years and had brought healing to many patients.

After his retirement he struggles with prostate cancer, but had managed to stay active and enjoy his life of retirement spending time with his wife, sons, daughter, and grandchildren.

At our last visit he had just celebrated his 92nd birthday. There is no doubt that his attitude and, his faith in a higher power __ notwithstanding a compromising and debilitating terminal disease illness __ contributed to his long life through facilitation of the applied power of positive thinking.

The doctor friend's terminal illness is an unforeseen circumstance over which he had little control. Nevertheless, it is a case of positive endurance, illustrating powerful testimony in support of *the applied power of positive thinking.*

*Name withheld for confidentiality

CHAPTER 17

Respect; Self / Others

Respect is a strong word: Webster's Dictionary defines respect as: To *"… esteem or admiration; consideration; example: a respect for power."*

Respect begins with one's self. If there is no respect for one 's self then it obviously follows, that one cannot respect another.

Subsequently, when there is no respect on either side, when individuals feel strongly about a circumstance, situation, of specific subject, either party may feel led to believe that, they have *carte blanche* to say or do whatever they want to do, or say.

Nothing could be farther from the truth. In fact, the truth of the matter is, one is judged by their words. It is assumed that, a person usually thinks what they say, and say what they think.

Breaking down that statement indicates, an individual usually knows what they are going to say *before* they say it.

There is an old Proverb which states: *"Put brain in gear before opening mouth."*

This appears to be a wise saying; words or actions can never be recalled. The bottom line is, the person being disrespectful to someone else is invariably the loser, and brings down insult upon them, with little, or no injury other than verbal, to the intended victim; the individual showing disrespect has only hurt themselves.

The wise individual, who is disrespectful to another, can redeem themselves by simply apologizing using *the applied power of positive thinking*

Vignette:

At the time this book was being written an honor student had been beaten to death by rival gang members in the city of Chicago. It was later learned, the reason for his death was simply because he would not agree to join a gang. The murder weapon was not a gun or knife; it was a piece of timber; a railroad tie.

What is the message? The message is clear: there was no respect shown to the victim by either of the rival gang members. Worse, neither of the rival gangbangers respected the decision by the Honor student to not join a gang. The only grain of respect shown was, by the Honor student; respecting himself in refusing to be intimidated into becoming a gang member even under the threat of loss of life, by being beaten to death.

This is an extreme example; it is not intended in way to encourage an individual, to be a stand-up person, by exercising their rights, at the cost of death.

Rather, the strength gained by respecting one's self, and by exercising one's rights, is strongly supported, however, it is better to be safe than sorry by applying sound value judgment and *the power of positive thinking.*

*Name withheld for confidentiality

CHAPTER 18

Claiming Responsibility

"It's not my fault!" is a common statement of denial from someone who may have had a finger pointed at them when something they may have been involved with goes awry or fails.

Fair or not, the reality is if, and when an individual is directly involved in a situational failure they are, obviously partially __ if not fully __ to blame, depending on the facts of the matter reveal, for that particular failure.

Shirking, or denying responsibility is the pattern of mankind.

For those who believe in Divine Intervention, the Holy Scriptures reveal the enemy Satan came in the form of a serpent into the Garden of Eden and tempted Eve to disobey and defy God's Commandment of *"Do not to eat of the fruit of the tree of knowledge."* The implied intent of the enemy Satan was to convince Eve that, God lied when he told her she would die if she ate the fruit. The story goes that he told Eve, *"If you eat of the fruit you would be as wise as God."* Genesis 3:4-5 (Paraphrase).

After much back and forth banter Eve gave in to temptation and ate of the fruit. The *Scripture reveals that "Immediately Eve's eyes were opened and she knew she was naked."*

It goes on to say that *"She then offered the fruit to Adam and, that he also ate of the fruit."* Genesis 3:6.

It is interesting to note that Adam took and ate the fruit quickly and willingly. He did not argue with Eve, and neither did he discipline or scold her for disobeying the command of their Creator; God. Conversely, Eve *had* argued with the serpent (Satan).

The Scripture reveals that later, when God came to the Garden to have fellowship with Adam and Eve they were nowhere to be found. Of course, since God is omniscience (all knowing) God already knew *where* they were and that both of them had disobeyed him, nevertheless, he called out to Adam: *"Adam, Adam, where are you?"* Adam replied, *"Over here Lord; we are naked and we are hiding ourselves." (Paraphrase)* They both were literally trying to hide from God. God asked, *"How do you know you are naked?"* Adam replied, blaming first God, and then Eve for beguiling (tricking) him into eating the forbidden fruit. His answer: *"That woman, who you gave me..."* He blamed God for his giving him the woman (Eve). He then went on to blame Eve, who by implication not only betrayed and disobeyed God, but he also blamed Eve by implying that Eve had also betrayed and, tricked him. Genesis 3:12.

The bottom line: Adam failed to accept responsibility, for his own weak-kneed action of betraying and disobeying God, by yielding to personal temptation, (regardless of whatever influence caused him to do it).

The action by Adam is called *"passing the buck;"* people have been doing it ever since Adam invented the excuse.

It appears to the author that, shirking responsibility, and passing the buck dismisses the "old school" line of reasoning and, thinking, i.e. *"do the crime; do the time,"* and for receiving appropriate punishment for violating the law, when an individual is directly responsible for their actions with good, bad, indifferent, or criminal behavior.

In other words, *when you are wrong; you are wrong.* There is no gray area between "right" and "wrong" action; it is black and white, in spite of the perception of some.

Therefore, when an individual commits a voluntary act of behavior, right or wrong, they are responsible, and should claim the action and confess the act, if in fact, the act is contradictory to the mores, folkways, and traditions of society, or violates the law of the land.

Unfortunately, this is *not the norm* for the socially deviant; they do not use a yard-stick to compare their actions to others, or to measure their own actions.

What *is* the yard-stick measure? Simple: as previously stated; the mores, folkways, and traditions of society, combined with common sense.

An individual who neglects or refuse to claim or accept responsibility for their actions, and are prone to shift blame to someone else, follows a pattern of "the least path of resistance." If one can shift blame away from themselves __ in their own mind __ they feel blameless, and vindicated.

There is a TV Program called "Bait Car," which focuses on car theft. The enforcement agencies plant a "bait car," after a "mock traffic stop of a disguised police officer, (who is allegedly taken away to jail). The "bait car" is usually a new luxury car, such as a Cadillac Escalade, left parked with a door open, keys in the ignition, and sometimes with the engine running).

The temptation for the criminal element is overwhelming; many times after observing the bait car (unbeknown to them) they facilitate a "theft" by getting in the vehicle and driving away. This is the trap law enforcement has set; the criminal gets caught in the trap; (can't get out of the vehicle due to law enforcement shutting down the engine and locking the doors). The criminal is arrested on the spot.

This actual episode is included to document just how individuals with criminal thinking backgrounds attempt to "pass the buck," in order to get off the hook, and avoid punishment for their crime.

The façade gamut of excuses and, "passing the buck" ranges from statements like *"the person who owns the car asked me to move it,"* to *"I was planning to take it to the local police station."*

A more innocent example of "passing the buck" can be observed when encountering a "newly hired" employee in a department store. The "new hire," who seeks to avoid responsibility of helping a customer find an item of merchandise in the store. The statement often heard is, *"I'm a new employee; I don't know,"* or, *"That's not my department."*

How does one assume self responsibility, and claim responsibility, when an error, mistake, wrong decision occurs, without blaming others, and avoid claiming responsibility by saying, *"It's not my fault?"*

A great question; it deserves a truthful answer. The answer would be: *"It has to be born in the spirit of honesty."*

Without the dynamic of honesty the tendency to give in to temptation becomes overwhelming and, the act of doing the "right thing" never happens and, the opportunity to facilitate and lost forever is ***the applied power of positive thinking.***

Vignette:

*Greg Brown, a young man in his late twenties, in Los Angeles, California, had recently lost his job due to his company downsizing. He was married with an 11 month old infant son. Unable to find employment he was forced to use credit cards to pay the rent and provide a meager living for his new wife and son.

Discouraged but not defeated, he was encouraged by family and friends to start a land- scape gardening business. He already owned a pick-up truck so he used a credit card, invested in a power mower, edger, and grass / leaf blower. The credit cards were slowly becoming maxed out. He knew he would soon have to start earning money or face bankruptcy.

Driving through the city looking for potential gardening customers he turned the corner to a new thoroughfare and noticed a bag lying in the street. He watched other cars swerving to avoid hitting the bag and drive on.

Always the curious type Greg pulled over his pickup and parked. Avoiding traffic he walked to the bag, picked it up, and walked back to his pickup He noticed a name imprinted on the canvas bag identifying it as armored car company property. Examining the bag closer he noted that the bag was sealed with a lead seal. He grabbed a pair of side-cutter pliers from the glove compartment and cut open the seal. To his great surprise he discovered stacks of twenty-dollar bills. His hands were shaking when he finished counting the stacks; there was twenty-thousand dollars.

Greg's mind was racing; was this answer to prayer? He asked himself. A voice seemed to say to him "You can pay off all your bills; finders, keepers." His mind continued to race: his mouth was dry. He put his head against the steering wheel; he broke out in a cold sweat.

Greg was not a very religious man but he remembered words his mother had used over and over as he was growing up." Always "do unto others as you would have others do unto you," she would say.

Greg knew what he had to do. He started the engine, pulled away from the curb and drove to the nearest police station. Taking the bag into the station he told the desk sergeant that he wanted to turn in a bag of money he had found.

The police notified the armored car company who immediately wanted to know "who" the finder was. They were so pleased to have the money returned they rewarded Greg with 10% of the money he turned in, or $3,000.

The armored car insurance company was so overwhelmed with Greg's honesty that they notified the press and local TV station that ran stories commending Greg for his honesty.

An interesting note: None of the bills were marked; if Greg had not turned in the money no one would have ever known about his find or, have been able to trace the lost currency.

But Greg's conscience would have known.

This vignette illustrates two dynamics: One, honesty is always the best policy and, two, it clearly illustrates that temptation *can be* overcome by facilitating *the applied power of positive thinking.*

There you have it: it is almost a "given" in our worldly society today; pass the buck, attempt to shirk responsibility, and shift the blame.

This vignette vividly points up the failure of some, and the claiming of responsibility by others in accepting responsibility for their actions, and the importance of obtaining a desired end result, by facilitating ***the applied power of positive thinking.***

CHAPTER 19

Help *Is* Available

Someone has said, *"You can't help somebody who doesn't want to be helped."*

This is a true statement. However, there are those who claim you can "force treat" person to be successfully helped. To prove the point that individuals cannot be successfully "force treated" we use the example of an addict.

It is a well known fact in the psychotherapeutic arena that, addiction __ regardless of the type; alcohol, prescription drugs, street drugs, or any other abused substance __ effective treatment cannot start unless and until, an individual recognizes and own up to the fact, that they are an addict and wants help.

Support of this hypothesis begs the question: How *can* help be provided to an addict who is focusing only on where the next "fix" or "drink" is coming from, and will take any action to satisfy that craving including burglary, extortion, or robbery, up to and including murder.

Once an individual faces the reality of their addition __ and admits to being an addict __ they have taken the first step toward getting help through successful counseling treatment.

It would appear that there is a foregone conclusion a sound mind would reach: those who do not want help, simply *cannot be helped.*

Conversely, those who face the reality of addiction and want help can most assuredly be helped; help *is* available. This holds true not only for the addict, but for others who may be experiencing other types of life issues or problems, i.e. persons facing familial issues, financial struggles, marital discord, and sexual issues, etc.

There are literally 1000's if not tens of 1000's of available qualified, private practice counselors, substance abuse counselors, financial consultants, marriage / family therapists, bereavement counselors, psychotherapists, group counselors, intervention therapists, and other professional clinicians.

Therefore, for those who realistically want help, help is available. Not only is help available for those seeking help, but the facilitation of *the applied power of positive thinking* can, and has, been highly successful as a treatment modality.

In support of this position a Vignette is presented which profoundly demonstrates a successful end result, brought about through facilitating the ***applied power of positive thinking.***

Vignette:

At age 12 Jamie started running with the wrong crows at school. He was introduced to marijuana and became a habitual abuser. He had long been told by friends' __ and some relative's __ *"that there is nothing wrong in using marijuana because, there is no lasting harm to the body or brain and, that it was widely accepted as a social drug like smoking cigarettes or drinking alcohol."*

With this stamp of approval Jamie was eager to *"try marijuana to see what it could do for me."*

His choice placed him on a slippery slope; the more he used, the more he wanted and, soon the "kick" he was getting from "weed was not enough." He began experimenting with other type street drugs; first Marijuana, then cocaine and methamphetamines.

By the time he reached high school he began cutting classes and, his grades started sliding, from a strong B to D's and F's. His parents were baffled; this was atypical behavior for a son who had loved school and had received high marks. The parents conference with the school counselors and finally learned that Jamie had become a drug addict at age 16.

The parents were connected to a local church and they turned to their pastor for counsel.

They indicated to the pastor that Jamie would *"not listen to them anymore, gave them empty promise to quit using but, went right back to the addiction."*

In the interim, Jamie had received barely passing grades but, had managed to graduate high school and would soon celebrate his eighteenth birthday. He had told the parents that *"when I (he) reached 18 I (he) am going to move out"* (of the parents home) and *become a beach bum. Then I (he) can do what I (he) want to do; nobody is going to tell me what to do."*

The pastor suggested to Jamie's parents that they conduct an 'intervention' with a qualified counselor where all of Jamie's family would be present to tell him how much they loved him and, at the same time, hated what he was doing to himself with drugs. And that, during the intervention each parent and sibling, and loved one would explain to Jamie that they were not going to support him anymore and, would refuse to connect with him, unless he agreed to go into a rehabilitation program.

The parents contacted a counselor who conducted intervention therapy programs and arranged to set up a meeting with family members and ask Jamie to attend the meeting without revealing to him the purpose.

Long story short; Jamie reluctantly attended the intervention session, broke down in tears and, agreed to go away with the therapist to a rehabilitation center located in the state of Arizona for a six month rehabilitation program.

The good news is, Jamie completed the rehabilitation program and has now been clean and sober for one year. This is a case where there was willing consent by Jamie who wanted to be helped. Obviously, if Jamie had not of consented to getting help he would have continued to abuse drugs and would still be an addict.

This vignette clearly demonstrates that in order for an addict to change, they have to want to change.

In Jamie's case, the desire and need was there; the fact that, the parents and family members were not willing to give up on him enabled Jamie to make a wise decision and, empowered him to follow their suggestion due to their concern and love for him.

While subtly used, the fact is not lost and must be credited, at least in part, for action motivated by the parents and family members.

Their action was strengthened by their willingness to facilitate *the applied power of positive thinking*.

*Name withheld for confidentiality

CHAPTER 20

Getting Professional Help

What motivates an individual to seek out professional help? Answer: There are several dynamics which motivates an individual to find counseling through a professional therapist.

Those dynamics are listed, as follows:

1. When an individual's ability to think cognitively and independently...
2. The feeling of being overwhelmed and, on overload due to issues that are seemingly unresolved, causing a sense of hopelessness and helplessness...
3. Low confidence, low self-esteem...
4. Inferiority complex causing negative thinking vs. positive thinking...

Positive Steps to Achievement:

ATITUDES

1. Desire / Goal
2. Making a Plan
3. Motivation through Inspiration

4. Moving Forward (drive)
5. Successful Accomplishment

Positive Steps for Maintaining Achievement:

ATITUDES

1. Associate With Positive People
2. Avoid Negative People
3. Look for Positive Dynamics:

    (a) Contrast / Compare: ½ Empty Vs ½ Full Glass
    (b) Contrast /Compare: Hole in Donut Vs Delicious Donut

4. Look for Ways to Compliment Others: Example: *"How nice to see you, Ann; your beautiful smile continues to be very contagious."*
5. Use Self Affirmations, i.e. Example: *"Every day, in every way, I'm getting better and stronger."*

Vignette:

A Vignette is provided to demonstrate how a 39 year old female, who had recently been abandoned and divorced by her husband for another woman, after 20 years of marriage, believed herself to be at the end of her rope, eventually sought professional help.

For several years Joan had suspected that her husband Ken was cheating on her. She had discovered lipstick on his shirt collars, a plane ticket with a female's name on it in his suit pocket, (who the husband claimed was a colleague he had traveled to a company conference with, who had asked him to hold on to her ticket, which he did, and he forget to give back the ticket before leaving the airport).

She also remembered that there had been other signs, like late hour telephone calls to his cell phone, home late arrivals from his work place, etc. Finally, Ken confessed that, there was *"another woman,"* and he told Joan, he *"wanted a divorce."*

Joan was devastated; a professional medical person, as a Registered Nurse, she worked long 12 hour shifts at the hospital and had forced herself to dismiss the tell-tale signs of infidelity evidenced by her husband. She wanted to give him the benefit of the doubt. But now it seemed to her like the roof had caved in.

Upon learning of her husband's request for "divorce" Joan had contacted a family attorney who advised her to, *"Let the husband file for the divorce."* When Joan presented this information to her husband he was anxious to please; Ken immediately filed for a divorce.

Joan was reflecting on her situation and became very depressed. She lost her appetite, couldn't sleep well, and started losing weight. She found her concentration was affected and, she became even more depressed because, she knew she needed full concentration to perform her nursing duties effectively. Suicidal ideations started creeping into her thinking.

Joan confided in her supervisor, who was also a personal friend. The friend encouraged her to *"don't give up; keep a positive attitude"* and, suggested Joan find a psychotherapist and schedule an appointment to receive some one-on-one therapeutic counseling. Joan took her nursing friend's suggestion, received a referral, from the Employee Assistance Program through her work, and scheduled an appointment.

It took several months of counseling for Joan to move from the denial, to acceptance stage that her marriage had failed. At first she had blamed herself, for circumstances leading up to the divorce, thinking that due to her long hour work schedule she had neglected her husband Ken. As she continued to talk through the circumstances in counseling she came to fully realize that, she had been the faithful one. That it had been Ken who was the cheater and violator of their 20 year old marriage vows.

Today, three years later, through effective professional counseling and supportive co-workers and friends, Joan has successfully moved through her pool of pain. At her hospital work place, she subsequently met, fell in love with, and married a young Medical Doctor, and has rebuilt her life, all because a friend introduced her to *the applied power of positive thinking.*

*Name changed for confidentiality

PART II

RELATIONSHIPS: The Marital Dyad; the Nuclear Family

Preface

After the marriage, when the honeymoon is over: Whereas, before the marriage, as a single individual the only person you had to be concerned about was YOU; There is now a 180 Degree turn about.

The thinking has to change: You now need to think for TWO!

1. Whenever you go...
2. Whatever you do...
3. Wherever you go...
4. Whatever you want life to be like...

You now must, necessarily **INCLUDE** your marriage partner.

No more contact with:

1. Old flames…
2. Former lovers…
3. No more affairs…
4. No more "flings"…
5. No more "seed-sowing"…

You now **BELONG TO** your marriage partner!

The marriage partner is owed your:

1. Commitment…
2. Your Faithfulness…
3. Your marriage vow of: **"…forsaking all others for you alone, until separated by death."**

Subjects to avoid in marriage:

1. "You said…"
2. "She said…"
3. Disrespect; **treat each other as an honored guest in your home.**
4. Avoid **ANY CONTACT** with former girl friends / boy friends, lovers, or sweethearts
5. Always be truthful; **AVOID LYING** to one another.

The Holy Scriptures say: *"…your sins will finds you out."* Numbers 32:23.

CHAPTER 21

Parenting

My wife and me, and the baby; now the thinking perception necessarily includes three persons: not me, myself, and I, rather, mommy, daddy and baby makes three.

Whereas, prior to marriage, as a single person, attention only had to focus on one individual. The act of meeting, falling in love, and marrying, now necessitates conscious awareness and thinking about someone, other than self.

Every facet of life now has to be considered from a plural perspective. The "I" becomes a "we;" not any easy adjustment. It takes time, effort, and energy to re-educate to the plural thinking process and, to form a mindset including a marriage partner.

However, the average couple chooses to have children early on in their marriage.

The expression has been heard: *"Have your children while young, and grow up with them."* While this may appear to be sound reasoning, it too often becomes cloudy thinking. Becoming a parent is the single biggest change in a couple's life-style. In the first few years of marriage the couple is getting acquainted; getting to know one another.

The transition into marriage and, now having to be thinking about two people is mild, compared to suddenly having to think about *three* people. The adjustment process becomes complicated and exacerbated when compounded with an un-expected pregnancy and, the imminent birth of a child.

The still "new" marital relationship is placed under major stress and, heavy obligation and responsibility, by the seemingly, never-ending needs and, demanding care of an infant. Demands which interrupt the "norm" of the husband and wife, i.e. 2, and 3 AM feeding, diapering, burping and, rocking back to sleep, takes a toll on the marital relationship, especially when there is a working mother and, when the parents are trying to equally share the parenting responsibilities.

The responsibility of parenting can be both a blessing and a curse, even for marriages which are solidly founded and have endured for two or more years. Bringing children into a new marital relationship __ before husband and wife have become fully acquainted with each other __ is not always fair to the child and, certainly not fair to the parents.

Much planning by husband and wife is needed in order for parenting to be a joyful, happy, and fulfilling experience. Time and appropriate planning by both parents provides opportunity for designing a bedroom, buying a crib, and other needed furnishings. During the pregnancy the results of a sonogram determines sex and, provides opportunity for the mother-to-be to buy an appropriate infant wardrobe, toys, diaper bag, and to stockpile diapers.

Each purchase becomes an accomplishment in anticipation of the "blessed event." This is possibly the most exciting time for both-parents-to-be, especially the expectant mother. The focus of both parents-to-be in preparation for parenthood ought to center on making appropriate decisions and learning how to agree, even if it is learning how to disagree, agreeably. An ideal situation, during the pregnancy, is provided early on for the expectant parents to start practicising harmony in decision making.

Provided that appropriate planning has been done, when the "blessed event" occurs the transition from not being a parent, to becoming a parent, is far less difficult. The "blessed event" can be accepted more readily as a "quasi-normal" happenstance.

It is important for new parents to know that, there is no "right way," or "wrong way" to simply be a "good parent." Thousands of books have been written on "Parenting," however, the bottom line is, no one can tell you exactly "how to" be a "good Parent."

Parenting has to be "learned" by hands on doing.

Grandparents, relatives, friends, and co-workers can all share their parenting experience with you, but when all is said and done, and discussion stops, a parent has to learn *how* to "do it my (their) way."

Who can tell you *"how to"* quiet a baby at 3 AM? This will happen frequently.

The following Vignette will help in answering that question.

Vignette:

The advice from a pediatrician may seem cold, cruel, and unprofessional; however, it was sage advice and exactly what my wife and I needed to hear.

This pediatrician told my wife and me some "shocking" facts concerning our first baby daughter who always chose the wee hours of the morn to start crying and only walking the floor with baby on the shoulder seemed to appease her.

The pediatrician gave the following strong advice:

"If she is not hungry, sick, soiled, or wet, put her back in the crib and let her cry."

The first time we followed his advice and *"Put her back in her crib and let her cry,"* she cried herself to sleep in about 30 minutes. The sound of her crying was nerve wrenching but she did, in fact, fall fast asleep.

The second time we *"Put her in her crib and let her cry,"* she cried for about 15 minutes.

Subsequently, each time we let her cry herself to sleep the time got less and less.

We learned a valuable lesson as parents; trust your pediatrician, he knows what he is talking about. He had told us, if the baby is *"not sick, soiled, or wet, then she is pulling the wool over your eyes;"* he was right.

We "learned" parenting on the first baby and how to enjoy; we fully enjoyed her siblings; blessings come in small packages.

Parenting is a blessing; learn and enjoy.

CHAPTER 22

Tough Love

A Clinical Psychologist wrote a book a few years ago in which he "coined" the phrase "Tough Love."

The work primarily deals with parents vs. teen sons and daughters exhibiting deviant behavior, or family members with unacceptable behavior. The "Tough Love" concept encouraged compassionate but firm refusal to become an enabler by accepting, condoning or overlooking, what would normally be called deviant, unacceptable, negative and sometimes abusive behavior from teen sons, daughters, and family members.

An illustration for this work; *"The applied Power of Positive Thinking,"* a true story about the foster son of an acquaintance to the writer, is presented as a Vignette.

Vignette:

A young man we will call *David was 12 years old and had been abandoned to Foster Care by divorced parents. He had ultimately become a foster child placed in a single mother parent's home. The single mother was also rearing a 6 year old biological daughter whose full custody she had been awarded at the time of divorce from a drug abusing addicted husband.

David was a very real challenge; the foster mother's discipline was laughed off with words of contempt, i.e. *"go ahead and ground me, it won't make any difference I'll just break the ground rule anyway and do whatever I please."*

The foster mother reports that David would steal money from her purse, go to a pornographic video store buy, (and steal), pornographic videos, then come home to watch them in front of the 6 year old female biological daughter. He also stated he *"hated school,"* and would cut classes.

The foster mother reported David's deviant behavior to the foster care agency. She was given an option: Relinquish foster care assignment and return David to the foster care agency for future placement, or alternatively, remain the foster care parent and work with David.

The foster mother was in a quandary; between a rock and a hard place. She didn't approve of David's inappropriate behavior and the bad influence he was having on the biological daughter but, at the same time she had empathy, concern and compassion for David as to what would happen if she returned David to the foster care agency.

The foster mother consulted and conference with her pastor and a clinical psychologist. Both offered essentially the same solution, i.e. continue trying to work with David with certain stipulations and boundaries:

The reasoning behind their suggestions was based on David's behavior of "acting out" his feelings of anger, and frustration, in coming from a broken home environment with abusive and divorced parents who failed to show their love, and the ultimate abandonment by his biological parents.

The pastor and psychologist agreed that David's unacceptable behavior of "acting out" his feelings stemmed from a hidden agenda of:

1. Parental rejection, and
2. A desire on David's part in wanting attention and recognition, whether for good or bad behavior
3. David's "acting out" behavior was a defense mechanism used by David in an attempt to shelter him from biological parent rejection

The suggestions offered two solutions: A and B

Solution A

1. Have a heart-to-heart talk with David and show him your concern, love, and compassion
   Reinforcing the reason you initially invited him into the home
2. Outline and put in place firm house rules with disciplinary consequences for breaking of the rules
3. Reinforce that fact that, disciplinary consequences for breaking of the house rules are not intended for punishment rather, as a result of your love in wanting David to learn that, you want David to learn to do the "right thing," and that, when rules are broken discipline is a consequence
4. Set boundaries for what in acceptable and unacceptable behavior
5. Rewards for ongoing acceptable behavior, i.e. a movie, pizza, etc.

In summary, if Solution A was ineffective, move to Solution B:

Solution B: Tough Love

1. To compassionately but with confidence let David know going forward the disciplinary path for him was that, he must necessarily follow the house rule and set boundaries
2. To accept responsibility for his actions
3. To admit when he broke the house rules and accept the disciplinary consequences
4. To take away privileges as a result of his breaking the rules or moving outside the set boundaries such as no television, no video games, etc. for a certain time

As an adjunct to either Solution A or B, it was suggested that:

David get involved in the foster mother's church youth group program activities, where he could be accepted as an equal, and engage his interest and unscheduled time to consume his energy.

Long story short, the foster mother conference with David reassuring him he was wanted as a part of the family and she asked him to partner with her to help him improve his behavior. With tears in his eyes David embraced the foster mother with a hug and promised *"to do better."*

Within a month David's behavior changed; he responded to the terms *"concern, compassion, and care,"* and agreed to *"try harder."*

Through the influence of the church youth group leader, pastor, and foster mother David came to his young adult senses, apologized for his aberrant behavior, asked forgiveness and promised to put forth effort to become a better team player and family member.

Fast forward: Now David is in Junior High school. His grade level went from a "C" to "B." His behavior has remarkably improved earning him a "Student Citizen Of The Month" Award.

David now says, *"I like school."*

This is a classic example of how successful end results can be achieved, through facilitation of "tough love" and ***the applied power of positive thinking.***

CHAPTER 23

Respect – Self and Others

Self

Definition: Respect: *"esteem or admiration, consideration;"* as defined by the New International Standard Webster's Dictionary.

The Holy Scripture admonishes mankind to "love your neighbor as you love yourself."

For believers in a Higher Power it is obvious that, the Intelligent Designer knew that with each design creation the designee was going to love itself; that was the logical assumption.

When the word "respect" is substituted for the word "love" a clearer picture emerges. Subsequently, the admonition *"…love your neighbor as you love yourself"**literally means to love (respect) yourself, not to be *"in love with yourself,"* rather, to respect yourself with integrity, truthfulness, and dignity. *Matthew 19:19 et al.

There was a time when a verbal promise, with a handshake, sealed a deal or contract. Today written contracts with witnesses and notarized documents appear to be the norm for conducting any type of business relationship. The underlying cause for the perceived need for protection stems from the threat of being sued or swindled.

It appears that the dynamic of trust has disappeared; the mind set is, *"you can't trust anyone."* The stark truth surges to the forefront; reality kicks in and paranoia captures an individual's mind.

Suddenly, an individual comes to grips with a perceived truth: "even I can't be trusted; I can't trust myself." Rational cognition seems to have flown out the window until the individual recognizes his perception is faulty; cloudy thinking has influenced belief and he comes to his senses and again believes in individual worth.

The rational cognition begins to reshape the thinking process and affirmations reinforce the positive belief system. The thinking begins to change, i.e. *"I am able;" "Everyday in every way, I am getting better and stronger." "I am an over comer; I can, I will."*

Positive thinking replaces the negative mind set and an individual begins to gain new value judgment and to recognize the value of their own worthiness. To use a biblical phrase, *"As a man (person) thinks in his heart, that so he is."* Proverbs 23:7.

Subsequently, the thought being, *"What you say, is what you think; what you think is what you become, until you decide to change."*

The individual has experienced a new level of *self-respect* through a self-realization awakening; a "new you," emerges having experienced a "new birth."

Vignette:

At age 15 Tyrone was no stranger to run-ins with the police. At such an early age his juvenile rap sheet included shoplifting, burglary, and truancy. He now sat in the high school principal's office accompanied by the principal and the school police officer waiting for his mother to arrive for a disciplinary conference.

Tyrone had been "caught" smoking weed in the men's restroom with one of his so-called-school buddies. He showed little remorse for his behavior when faced by his mother who had just been ushered into the principal's office.

She silently stood in front of him; her look of disappointment spoke volumes breaking through Tyrone's somber expression. Suddenly, tears glistened in his eyes; he abruptly buried his face in his hands. Silent sobs shook his shoulders. In a broken voice he was able to say three words: *"Mother, I'm sorry."*

After conferencing with the principal and school police officer Tyrone received a written disciplinary ticket for a juvenile court appearance and was placed on probation for six months by the principal. He was released to the custody of his widowed, single parent mother.

On the drive home Tyrone regained his composure and continued to apologize for his behavior. His mother simply said, *"We'll talk about it when we get home."*

Upon arriving at home his mother and he headed for the den to discuss his behavior. Notwithstanding the fact that his mother had to take a half-day off from work __ losing much needed salary __ she maintained calm and maintained her peace in dealing with Tyrone. She pointed up her disappointment over his unacceptable behavior and the fact that his juvenile record would be a disadvantage to his future unless he started taking responsibility for his actions and behavior. She also pointed out to him how commendable his behavior had been up until a year and a half ago. Reminding him of how he had been an honor student and had received student of the month on several occasions.

His mother encouraged him to think back to those better times and requested him to make a greater effort to again become the excellent student he once had been.

In a gentle caring and loving way his mother promised him that, if he would stay out of trouble for one year she would reward him by helping him obtain a driver's license when he turned 16.

She continued, "On the other hand, if your abhorrent behavior continues you will be grounded for two weeks and face stern discipline with suspended privileges, i.e. no TV Games, no TV, no Cell Phone, and no sleep-over's at friends homes.

With tears spilling down her face she went on to say *"Since your father passed you are the only man in the home. I would like to look up to you as the "man of the house" as a role model for your little sister and brother and to help them as they grow up."*

This approach by his mother seemed to deeply touch Tyrone's emotion. He embraced his mother with a hug, apologized again for his behavior, and promised he would *"try harder,"* and *"yes,"* he would like to become the *'man of the house.'*

A year and a half later Tyrone has been true to his promise. He now has his driver's license and uses his mother's car __ when she is with him __ to drive to the mall, movies, and other relatives homes.

This vignette is presented to demonstrate the "how to" apply a positive mental attitude to affect a calm spirit, and to stay in peace as evidenced by Tyrone's widowed, single parent mother.

This vignette remarkably demonstrates how successful end results can be captured though facilitating *the applied power of positive thinking.*

Others

How *does* one show respect to "others?"

Retuning to the **Definition** of Respect: *"esteem or admiration, consideration."* It would seem reasonable as a starting point to use the biblical admonition which states, *"Do unto others as you would have others do unto you."* Matthew 7:12.

Obviously, if others are treated by us, as we would like to be treated by them, we are half-way there to giving and showing respect for others.

Vignette:

I heard a story about a lady waiting at the airport. Her flight was delayed by a couple of hours. She browsed the gift shop, bought a book and a bag of chocolate chip cookies, and found a seat at the passenger boarding gate. She sat down and placed her purse and other items of stuff on the seat beside her.

A gentleman sat down next to her. She had finished reading the first chapter of the book when she noticed the man reach into the bag and help himself to a cookie. She tried to ignore his action but became more aggravated as the man continued to help himself to the cookies. When there was only one cookie left in the bag she wondered what the man would do. He took the cookie, broke it, and offered her half .She accepted the cookie trying hard to control her anger.

She was relieved when she heard her flight being called. After boarding the plane she fastened the seat belt and returned to reading her book. Suddenly she sneezed; her eyes began to water. She reached into her carry-on bag for a tissue and to her surprise discovered her unopened bag of cookies. She was glad that she had kept her cool but was very embarrassed and felt like a fool.

Although humorous, this is a prime example of how both parties controlled their emotions and claimed their peace, notwithstanding the fact that, they both were understandably aggravated and irritated and perhaps seething on the inside.

They didn't let the "outside" circumstances affect or influence the "inside" dynamic.

To bring about a successful solution, and to make the best of an uncomfortable and unpleasant situation, they had controlled their temper, "zipped their lip" and facilitated *the applied power of positive thinking.*

CHAPTER 24

The Marriage Trap; He Said, She Said

Recognition of an issue, or issues, by one spouse ___ without respect to the other ___ cause couples to fall into a "marriage trap."

Too often, when an issue does arise between marriage partners neither party sees the need to talk about the issue until the issue has grown in intensity to the point of volatile, verbal exchanges. When this happens low boiling points and short fuses cause the situation to go out of control.

A Vignette is presented here to underscore the validity of the foregoing statement.

Vignette

After 19 years of marriage a couple goes to a marriage therapist. The history session regarding the couples prevailing issues becomes a *'he does this,' 'she does that,'* confrontation with raised voices and out of control anger. Both marriage partners are struggling in facing the reality that their situation appears to be hopeless.

Using education, acquired skill, and years of experience in marriage counseling the therapist encourages the couple to put "all issues on the table."

When all of the issues are brought into focus the marriage therapist can now lead the parties to prioritize the issues and, at the same time, to sift and sort discarding non-essential issues.

The therapist then encourages the couple to individually personalize the issues __ one at a time __ as to "why" it is an issue to them. This is called "venting" and allows the individual to express their feelings surrounding the particular issue.

Once the issue has been "vented" the therapist then encourages the other party to respond to what they have just heard.

This provides opportunity for each marriage partner to "get in touch" with their own feelings; sometimes the issues being discussed by one party is "new information" to the other.

The reason being, the subject issue being discussed has been camouflaged and hidden behind loud and angry expressions. Therefore, when the "new information" is brought to the forefront __ with guidance from the marriage therapist __ it provides opportunity for rational discussion by both parties to "talk-it-out" and bring resolution.

By "talking through the issues," one at a time, the couple gains new insight into *why* their behavior, influenced by past issues, has affected their marriage.

It is interesting to note that, some people __ both male and female __ have made the statement, *"I will never get married because as a single person I can:*

1. *Go where I want to go...*
2. *Do what I want to do, and...*
3. *Be what I want to be*

Which is true; they have spoken the truth: As a single person there is only one person you are responsible for. You can...

1. Think only of yourself...
2. Plan only for you, and...
3. Have no one else to be responsible to, or for

Your life can become a whirlwind of boozing, tripping, drugging and sexing if you are of a mind to do so. Your life-style can be for you, a "Happy Merry-go-round."

Fortunately, for most, this life-style gets boring and old as interested individuals focus begins to shift from self to members of the opposite sex, and then to a life-mate; a soul-mate; Someone with whom common interests are shared beyond the dance floor and bedroom. One starts to look for a life-partner.

Then somewhere along the way on an enchanted evening the person perceived to be Mrs. or Mr. "Right" __ the man or woman of cherished dreams __ walks within flirting distance. And thus begins a romance like never before experienced; the Mrs. or Mr. Right is unlike any other person ever before met.

The mind forms the words; this is "it." In a normal and natural course of action it is recognized that days appear clearer and filled with rays of sunshine; nights are brighter and life appears to be sweeter.

With each new date the feeling of enchantment grows stronger. The thought occurs "this is the person I want to spend the rest of my life with." The budding romance has blossomed into Full bloom and "love" has struck a positive and consuming blow.

The question of "Should we get married?" is considered and the inevitable question of "Will you marry me?" is asked.

"Yes. I will marry you," brings stars to the eyes of the soon-to-be-married couple and in time wedding bells are ringing in the chapel; then the honeymoon.

Back to the Vignette: The couple referenced at the beginning of this vignette, with guidance from the marriage therapist, applied the dynamics outlined in **Chapter 12, Anger / Resolution: Giving / Receiving Apology & Forgiveness,** to their marital situation.

Through their desire and willingness to save their 19 year marriage, and their willingness to follow the step-by-step procedure illustrated in that chapter, they were able to move past their differences and resolved their major issues.

Going forward, they anticipate celebrating many more happy wedding anniversaries.

Here is yet another illustration of how a successful end result can be achieved through facilitation of *the applied power of positive thinking.*

CHAPTER 25

Take Charge; Stay in Control

Each and every time the author has interviewed individuals or couples for counseling it quickly becomes apparent that a situation or an individual is out of control.

Every individual facing a circumstance, issue, problem or situation has a story to tell. As a pastoral counselor and psychotherapist it has always been the practice to hear out both sides of every story; with couples by having an individual therapy session, and then together in conjoint therapy.

During the conjoint therapy session each individual was encouraged to share their issues _ perceived or otherwise __ with one another; the same information which had been shared with the therapist during the individual therapy session. In other words, to bring into focus, and put on the proverbial table, every factual dysfunctional issue, i.e. to conjointly explain every act of dislike, of disagreement, and subject of every argument.

Through the venting process anger was defused, low boiling points were elevated, and short fuses were made longer, thus, decreasing the chance for an immediate blow-up explosion.

One of the greatest assets an individual has available to them is self-control. A situation is either under control or out of control; there is no middle ground for control. Subsequently, being able to take charge of any given situation is very important, but that is only half of the equation; staying in control is the other half.

For example: in a marital relationship, where there is a sharp disagreement, it is equally important for each marriage partner to use a soft voice and calm spirit in approaching the subject for discussion. Obviously, neither party can control the other, therefore, it is extremely important for each to take charge of their own emotions and feelings, and stay in control during the discussion.

This is true even if the discussion becomes heated. By staying in control of self, both parties can come to an agreement; even if it is *agreeing to disagree, agreeably.* This allows the conversation to flow back and forth in a calm and peaceful manner.

It has been previously mentioned that sometimes, a marriage partner may be harboring a grievance for which the other partner is completely unaware. By taking charge and staying in control, any hidden or camouflaged issue can be brought to the surface and calmly discussed to a successful resolution.

The greatest potential possessed by an individual is the ability to unselfishly recognize their own mistakes. When this potential is blocked by one party, reasoning is abandoned and compromise is impossible

The best solution to resolving issues is self-control; the formula for successful resolution is to take charge and stay in control of any given situation.

Vignette:

Rose and Karl had been married just over two years when dissension started to cause cracks in an otherwise solid marriage. Karl was a restaurant manager and the position demanded excessive hours on the job and away from home.

Rose also worked as a Para-legal for an attorney but her work week was Monday through Friday 8 to 5. She was an only child, from an affluent family, and had been the apple of her parent's eye never wanting for anything as she grew up. To put it another way __ in her own words __ she was *"a spoiled brat."*

Karl and Rose both were aware of the demands from his employment when they met and started dating. Nevertheless, they didn't think the long hours would affect their relationship and, in fact, it didn't during the dating stage; they made time for each other.

Someone has said, "Love is blind" and this was certainly the case with Rose and Karl at least with regard to their ignorance and denial in believing long hours would not affect their relationship.

The romance evolved into what they both considered to be love, become engaged, and with the blessing of both sets of parents, ultimately married.

In the beginning Karl was fortunate in having a competent assistant manager who could relieve him every other evening and on alternate week-ends. That soon changed when his assistant was promoted to manager of another restaurant in the chain.

The assistant's replacement was a new-hire, with very little experience in traditional restaurant management, having been hired out of fast food employment. Subsequently, he could not be trusted to be fully responsible in Karl's absence, and at the end of the shift, due to inexperience, was not capable of closing the traditional restaurant.

Therefore, Karl had to necessarily work extended hours and extra week-ends. This left Rose at home alone. At first she didn't mind because she would call up girl friends and they would go to a movie or visit at either home watching TV or just talking.

This arrangement was great fun at first but soon became boring and same-oh, same-oh to Rose. This is when the dissension between Rose and Karl began. Rose didn't want to make a big deal out of it initially because Karl earned a very comfortable salary and she didn't want to rock the boat. However, as Karl was away from home working extended hours and increased week-ends Rose was compelled to complain.

Their relationship was now entering rocky ground. Arguments were becoming more frequent; tempers were flaring and flaming. The marriage they both believed had been made in Heaven was now fast becoming a Hell on earth.

By using skills they had acquired in their positions of employment they decided to take a rational approach to their situation. On Karl's next free week-end they planned a get-away to a local mountain retreat where they could be free from telephones, email, and other distractions.

Alone in the mountain cabin each acknowledged that they were mature, level headed adults. They agreed to follow some suggestions by a friend who was a marriage counselor. The friend had suggested they take a piece of notebook paper, draw a vertical line down the middle, and then, individually list the positive and negative effect of each issue which that person was concerned about.

In the order of importance the issues to be discussed and, talked through, are prioritized. The thought being, (the marriage counselor had said), by listing and prioritizing the issues, was to help them recognize that there were issues of insignificant importance that should be discarded, and to point up the really important issues which were affecting their marriage.

Each was to list, prioritize and discuss with the other, the important issues __ one at a time __ facing them, to bring each issue to a successful resolution.

Rose and Karl liked the suggestion and followed through on it consistent with the marriage counselor's suggestion.

Once having listed, and prioritized the issues Karl and Rose were amazed to see just how many of the issues they had perceived to be important were not. The exercise lasted for several hours until all of the important issues had been put on the table, discussed and resolved.

The most important issue facing Rose and Karl were his extended hours at work taking him away from home and the companionship of Rose. In discussing this particular issue Karl was suddenly inspired to offer a doable and workable solution. Facing Rose he said:

"Honey, I have a great idea. You have been spending time with some of your girl friends going to movies and so forth, why not bring your girl friend down to the restaurant one night a week for dinner and I could join you? And then, you could also come to the restaurant by yourself, for dinner one night a week and I could join you. How does that sound?" he asked.

"That would be a big help, Karl; it would also give me more of your sharing time even though you would be technically working," Rose replied, agreeing with the suggestion.

Karl and Rose left the mountain retreat happier than they had been for a long time. Not only had they saved their marriage, they had also learned how to approach seemingly impossible issues with solvable solutions.

This Vignette clearly demonstrates and illustrates how, doable and workable resolution can be achieved through facilitating ***the applied power of positive thinking***

CHAPTER 26

Putting *Down* Wife / Husband

There is nothing more devastating or hurtful to a marital relationship than when either marriage partner criticizes or "puts down" the other privately, but especially in public.

There is an old expression which asks the question, *"Why do we always hurt the ones' we love?"*

That's a fair question. Why do some marriage partners feel justified in "putting down" the one person they should love more than anyone else; their husband or wife?

There are numerous reasons: Not justifiable reasons, but never-the-less reasons.

Some of the most common are listed:

1. Putting down the marriage partner in order to (mistakenly) lift up self...
2. An attempt to place a "guilt trip" on the other to motivate action, i.e. lose weight, quit smoking, etc.
3. To call attention to self and gain recognition (bad recognition, but recognition)...
4. To control the other...
5. To produce an inferiority complex in other...
6. One marriage partner is ashamed of the other...

These are only a few of the many reasons which could be listed. Again, not credible or justifiable reasons; only in the mind of the criticizer.

Each of these most common "reasons" will be discussed in brevity. First of all:

1. **Putting down the marriage partner in order to (mistakenly) lift up self...**

It would appear that some have unwittingly jumped into a marriage out of guilt over a pregnancy or run-away-emotions and, in fact, now realize that they made a mistake and really didn't want to get married to this particular person. Therefore, without admitting the mistake (to them self) they attempt to off-set their (believed to be) faulty thinking by putting down the marriage partner. That is, putting the other down to lift up "self".

2. **An attempt to place a "guilt trip" on the other to motivate action, i.e. lose weight, quit smoking, etc.**

When one marriage partner doesn't like an undesirable habit such as smoking, drinking, over-eating, etc. attempts are made through criticism to "shame" the other partner into doing something about abandoning the habit (addiction) or to lose weight.

Unfortunately, the criticism often drives the one being criticized to do exactly the opposite. Instead of quitting smoking or giving up an addiction, or losing weight the one being criticized often over-indulges by eating too much, drinking too much, or over dosing with prescription or street drugs potentially causing death.

3. **To call attention to self and gain recognition (bad recognition, but recognition)...**

People from all walks in life crave attention and recognition; whether innate or a learned characteristic is uncertain. In any event, recognition (good or bad) is a human characteristic.

When one marriage partner feels inferior to the other there is a tendency to look for faults in the other. Subsequently, fault-finding becomes an obsession and the smallest fault becomes huge in the eye of the criticizer. With each new opportunity (whether private or in public) criticism is heaped upon criticism.

The monumental criticism is intended to make the one marriage partner look small, in the eyes of others, and to make the criticizer look large in their eyes.

4. **To control the other...**

For some control is a big part of their mental make-up. They don't feel comfortable unless and until they can influence the other marriage partner to do what they want them to do regardless of what that may be.

As the control exacerbates it becomes a form of "brain-washing" to the point where one marriage partner controls the mind of the other. As the control increases the independent thinking process of the other marriage partner diminishes and often becomes non-functional. That is to say, with complete control by one marriage partner over the other , the one being controlled will not act independently without instruction from the other.

5. **To produce an inferiority complex in the other...**

If a marriage partner feels inferior to the other for whatever reason, the one who feels inferior attempts to undermine the other, with harsh criticism, and transfer their inferiority complex to their partner. When the transfer is successful the one feeling inferior is happy, because they have brought the other down to their lever of inferiority.

6. One marriage partner is ashamed of the other...

Some marriages falter and fail due to either partner "letting themselves go" after the marriage. This is true for the female partner especially after pregnancy and giving birth. Too often the mother neglects her after pregnancy weight gain, fails to work-out at the gym, and in some case even continues to gain weight. The male partner no longer see the slim and trim partner he married and is tempted to let his eyes "stray" in admiring other females, and can lead to infidelity and affairs.

The male marriages partner is no longer proud to "show-off" his beautiful bride who is no wearing loose fitting garments to conceal her over-weight condition; in fact, he is ashamed of her. On the other hand, when the male partner neglects his physical appearance, lets his hair grow into a pony-tail, wears tattered jeans, sleeveless t-shirts and doesn't bathe regularly the female partner becomes less enchanted. The tall, thin, sleek handsome guy she married no longer exists; he has become a slob. The female partner is no longer proud of him; in fact, she is ashamed to call him "husband" and often says so in front of others. When she criticizes him for days he gives her the "silent" treatment.

Vignette:

Helen had never been interested in learning to cook alongside her mother in the kitchen. This character flaw carried over into her young adult years. At school she hated the home economics class and reluctantly participated in the baking and cooking sessions.

Not knowing how to cook wasn't a big deal to Helen as long as she lived at home and later living in the college dorm she took most of her meals in the school cafeteria and fast food restaurants. However, it did become a problem after graduating college and moving into an apartment to live alone.

Helen discovered eating out all of the time was very expensive and crimped her budget. So she began to buy TV dinners and easy to prepare food in the microwave. This appeared to be working but she found the food to be tasteless and unappetizing; not a good thing.

After graduation she started working in employment consistent with her major of gerontology; she loved working with older people. Hr new found employment was in an oncology medical clinic where the challenge was great but the salary was entry level.

In the first six months she met an RN named Ray. They appeared to establish professional rapport. Overtime they began having lunch together in the clinic cafeteria; soon after they began dating. Ray loved to eat and preferred gourmet food. Helen remained silent when Ray talked about food.

Eventually, Helen was compelled to engage in the food discussion. She honestly and readily admitted her inability as a good cook. Ray simply passed off her comment by saying, "Well, you can always learn."

Helen was offended by his remark but let it pass and didn't respond. She felt like he was rude and putting her down. Her memory flashed back to her reluctance to learn how to cook; she had not really changed her mind.

In spite of their food differences their romance blossomed. Ray was mentioning marriage frequently, notwithstanding the fact that, in mixed company Ray had been jokingly making negative comments about Helen's inability to cook. The remarks embarrassed her, and hurt her feelings, but she let the comments slide.

In the interim, Ray had asked her to marry him and she had accepted his proposal. Six months later they were married and established their residence. Almost immediately Helen's inability to cook became an issue. Ray loved to eat gourmet food; Helen was not a gourmet cook.

The issue exacerbated creating tension in the marriage. Ray insisted Helen enroll in a community college food preparation class and Helen resisted. Tension increased threatening break-up of the marriage.

Long story short; after a heart-to-heart talk ending with hugs and kisses Helen agreed to enroll in a food preparation class.

After one semester Helen discovered her reluctance to be in the kitchen cooking had dissipated; she actually began to enjoy cooking and looked forward to learning how to prepare some of Ray's favorite dishes.

Six months has passed and Ray and Helen have resolved their issues through concern, love for each other, and compromise.

Another victory facilitated by *the applied power of positive thinking.*

CHAPTER 27

The "Blame Game"

When things go wrong in a relationship the natural thing to do is to blame everyone and everything, except self, for the dysfunctional issue evolving from the broken relationship.

Invariably, the least path of resistance is adopted by one or both parties, in trying to absolve self-responsibility, or to shift the blame.

One of the best examples to illustrate the least path of resistance can be captured in using a styrofoam cup filled ¾ full with water.

Example: You can fill the cup ¾'s full with water, set it on a table, punch a hole in the side, and the water will run out down to the level of the hole. Thus, the water has traveled *"the least path of resistance."*

This example typifies what happens when either party in a relationship makes a mistake. Since no one likes to be wrong, and believe they make mistakes, the normal and natural tendency is to look to the other party to find fault or blame. Obviously, the easiest road to travel is to take the least path of resistance and blame the other party.

The most difficult __ but most appropriate __ action to take, is to claim responsibility for self actions. This is discussed in another chapter, **Chapter 18, Claiming Responsibilities; Not Blaming Others** which the reader may want to refer to.

As a marriage counselor and psychotherapist years of con-joint therapy with couples reveals that neither spouse likes to believe they are capable of making a mistake, or "screwing-up," or of simply being wrong.

Invariably, when a couple realizes there are irreconcilable differences, issues, or problems between them they are usually incapable of sorting out the facts and facing the reality of the differences.

Often a wife or husband will turn to an acquaintance, friend, co-worker, or relative." In order for them to retain the friendship, these folks will tell the counselee, exactly what they think they want to hear. Not a good idea. Someone has said, *"If you want bad advice, turn to an acquaintance, friend, co-worker, or relative."*

An attorney would tell you, *"If you choose to be your own lawyer, you have a fool for an attorney."* Therapists would probably not be so bold but would tell you, "When you have a problem or issue don't go to your friends; they will give you bad advice."

Why? Because, at the risk of being redundant, these folks will tell you what they think you want to hear to retain your friendship. They cannot be objective.

The very best person to turn to in an attempt to resolve differences and issues to a successful solution is a trained psychotherapist, pastoral counselor, or marriage counselor.

These professionals are educationally learned and experienced therapists in the art of counseling trained to be "active listeners," not to take sides, and able to guide the counselees through their difficulties for a workable doable, practical, and effective resolution. The best scenario is for both marriage partners to be in agreement to attend con-joint therapy sessions.

In con-joint therapy the therapist hears both sides of the couples issues or problems and is able through his/her education, knowledge, experience, and wisdom to place before the marriage partners viable and credible alternatives to choose from, and apply to the dysfunctional situation to bring about the desired resolution and reconciliation.

By pointing up several alternative choices the therapist facilitates different paths which can be followed in an attempt to bring about a successful end result. If one alternative does not work, by choice, the counselees can try another alternative path.

The wise therapist avoids giving advice and uses their education, knowledge, experience and wisdom to point out different doable, workable, credible and viable alternative paths to successful resolution.

The experienced therapist understands the reason for not giving advice: that is to say, if a therapist advices the marriage partners to "do this" or "that" and "this" or "that" isn't successful, and doesn't work out to resolution, then the counselees could, and often do, blame the therapist for "not knowing what they are talking about."

On the other hand, the wise therapist offers several alternative paths which could be followed to bring about the desired end result. The therapist would then ask the counselees *"Which of these alterative paths do you want to follow? What do you want to do?"* This places the responsibility of making a choice on the marriage partners.

This method of therapy allows the counselees to maintain their independence in decision making and, if the chosen alternative is unsuccessful, and does not work out, the therapist can guide the counselees to make another independent choice in choosing from the alternative solution path. The counselees can continue making independent decision in choosing from the alternative pool until a successful resolution is reached.

This type of con-joint couples therapy gives the counselees renewed confidence in knowing that they had a role in bringing forth successful resolution to their issues. It also starts to dissolve the blame, and to shift it in another direction away from the counselees causing the issue to simply be a subject for discussion.

When the focus is on the issue and relieving the dissension, the issue can be discussed objectively, outside the box so to speak; standing on the outside looking on the inside, rather than the opposite of standing on the inside, and looking on the outside. If this sound confusing just know, that's what therapy is all about; placing all issues on the table, allowing both parties to vent their feelings by discussing the issue(s), to that end of arriving at credible alternatives; alternatives which can be applied for successful achievement resolution.

Vignette:

Joe and Molly were struggling for self identity. Ever since their marriage four years ago they had tried desperately to maintain their independence. They kept separate checking accounts, went on separate vacations, and slept in separate beds in their bedroom.

This appeared to be all well and good until one of them, overstepped their boundary and, inadvertently stepped into the space of the other. That when tempers flamed and flared; the blame game started. They used a philosophy set to anger to reinforce their arguments against each other i.e. *"It's your fault!" "You said this,"* and *"You did that."*

Joe and Molly became willing participants in conjoint therapy. They agreed to objectively discuss the issues, notwithstanding the fact that the issues were, in fact, subjective.

This was the first step in achieving resolution to their differences and issues. The fact that they were deeply in love was a significant plus for them. Their anger over the differences had not robbed them of their individual dignity and respect for each other.

They were willing to openly discuss their differences and through conjoint therapy began to accept responsibility for their actions and behavior.

During the course of therapy, what had seemed like an insurmountable mountain to climb now began to look like a steep hill. Their willingness to openly discuss their issues and differences, and accept their responsibility with equal blame, became a catalyst in helping them to obtain successful resolutions.

Three years have passed since Joe and Molly stopped going to therapy. They appear to now be happier than they have ever been. They are looking forward to being parents; Molly is six months pregnant. Joe can hardly wait to become a dad.

What conceivably could have been a broken marriage with divorce, turned out to be a happily married couple enjoying each other's love.

This would never have happened without their willingness to adopt an attitude of "we can work things out," and by realistically facilitating *the applied power of positive thinking.*

CHAPTER 28

Permission: Giving; Receiving

Someone has said, *"It is better to give than to receive."* For the sake of argument, with regard to relationships, it depends on who you are talking to.

Someone else has said, *"All is fair in love and in war."*

For identity purpose, neither statement is totally accurate relative to this publication. In marital relationships it is never consistently just 50 -50%, that is, 50% for the one marriage partner and 50% for the other. As a matter of fact, Giving and receiving is variable and change from day to day, and situation to situation.

Compromise becomes the "key word" in successful marriage relationships.

For example: The husband may have to give 80% to the wife's 20% one day, and in the next it might be the wife giving 75% to the husband's 25%. There does not appear to be a constant in giving and in receiving.

It appears that the only "constant" is found in "change" as alluded to in **Chapter 15 Past – Present – Future – *Change***. The readers may want to review that chapter.

In short term marital relationships (less than 5 years) it is extremely important for each marriage partner to consult with their other half concerning any major decisions that affects both partners. After having discussion the party who is responsible for ultimately making the decision needs to ask and receive permission to act on behalf of both marriage partners.

By using this method and technique both partners are kept aware of (in the loop, so to speak), of all major decision making procedures and has, at least, discussed the subject to be dealt with and have offered their blessing by giving their permission for the decision to be made.

This is where the "key word" compromise comes into focus: Even if both partners don't specifically agree on issues, as to outcome, they can, at least, agree to disagree agreeably.

No where is it written that every marriage partner is going to harmoniously agree with every decision faced by the other marriage partner. It flies in the face of self-identity.

By nature, all or most of us, are independent to that end of, believing even when we are convinced to make a decision, or to agree with the other marriage partner making a decision, we like to think the decision we make is our own idea; that's human nature.

In fact, one marriage partner may not like the decision his/her partner is going to make. However, after equal discussion and careful consideration, she/he is willing to *compromise* because, she/he realizes the value of making a wise joint decision.

Vignette:

Initially Carla and Ron agreed on every decision which confronted them. As time passed and they become more comfortable and familiar with each other this began to change.

Under ordinary circumstances, when a marital relationship has a rock-solid foundation, this would have been a good thing. It would have indicated maturing to the point where they no longer believed it necessary to consult with each other on every little decision to be made.

Rather, that only a major decision continued to need joint consultation prior to the decision being made.

Carla and Ron's marital relations were not ordinary; suspicions of jealousy and mistrust had begun to creep in. Ron was coming home later and later from work; Carla was beginning to withhold sex from Ron claiming she was *"too tired."* This frustrated Ron and his suspicions grew. His thinking was, if she is not getting sex at home then, she must be getting it someplace else. Accusations soon became frequent.

It is a well know therapeutic fact that, when everything is going well in the sex department, other concerns fall by the wayside. However, when sex becomes an issue, it appears that everything else, regardless of how small, is exacerbated.

Carla denied any infidelity but the denial didn't seem to please Ron. The more he was denied sex the greater his suspicions.

Ron and Carla finally agreed to sit down and have a heart-to-heart talk about where their relationship was headed.

They confronted and discussed each issue: mistrust, jealousy and suspicions. By applying value judgment they were able to work through these issues and reconcile their differences, and ended their heart-to-heart talk with a hug and a kiss and promised each other they would *"try harder to be a better marriage partner, and do better."*

Five years later, Carla and Ron are still very much in love and are fully enjoying each other's companionship and company.

Another illustration of just how important it is to use good value judgment, clear-headed thinking, and to take charge of anger, and stay in control of emotions.

This Vignette typifies how desired, doable and workable end results can be accomplished through facilitation of *the applied power of positive thinking.*

CHAPTER 29

Setting Boundaries

When we travel to farm areas and view fields and pastures we can see miles and miles of fencing setting boundaries for animals and livestock.

The fence serves a two-fold purpose; it keeps domestic live-stock inside the enclosure while keeping wild animal intruders outside the enclosure, thereby creating a boundary.

This analogy may appear to be juvenile and simplistic but it is realistic. The comparison can be paralleled to *Homo sapiens*; i.e. human beings.

While not restrained by physical boundaries, there are less tangible boundaries.

For example: Federal, State, City, and County __ considered to be laws of the land __ tell us how we can drive a vehicle; that we must have a driver's license; that we must have insurance; that we cannot legally drive under the influence of controlled substances, and on, and on. We are required by law to pay income tax, state tax, city tax, county tax, etc.

Subsequently, like it or not, we do have boundaries which have been established, over which we have no choice other than to choose to pay. This appears to be a biblical truth, as well. The Holy Scriptures admonishes us to *"render unto Caesar that which is Caesar's and unto God that which is God's."* Matthew 21:41, *et al*

However, the intent of this work is to discuss another type of boundary setting. Boundaries that pertain to children; employees; employers; schools and students; husbands, wives; and politicians.

Each of these areas will be discussed in brevity and the chapter on Boundary Setting will conclude with a positive example illustrated with a *powerful* Vignette.

THE DRIVER'S LICENSE:

The majority of states require a person to be 16 years of age (exception: some southern states) before they are eligible to obtain a learners permit to drive. In order for that permit to be legal a licensed driver has to be present in the vehicle while the minor is behind the wheel, learning to drive.

This practice continues until the teacher determines that the student driver to be competent enough to take and pass the driver examination conducted by the Department of Motor Vehicles (DMV).

After obtaining the driver's license the newly licensed driver has many boundaries set by the state, city, and county to control his driving behavior, to included having insurance, number of passengers in vehicle, use of safety belts by all inhabitants, etc. The boundaries set by the parents and school system becomes even more stringent.

From society's point or view these are good and positive boundaries which maintain safety and protect members of society at large.

INCOME TAX:

Federal and State income tax, social security deductions, etc. Are boundaries set in place by government agencies i.e. the IRS and State Income Tax Agencies.

The scenario: A student graduates high school or college and __ depending on what their personal perception is personally best for them __ and pursues employment in the workplace.

Regardless of whatever position or job they take they are necessarily bound by specific boundaries as to how much income tax they pay, how much for social security the employer deducts, and multiple other deductions over which the working individual has little or no control depending on the number of payroll exemptions claimed. These set boundaries are called "mandatory boundaries." There are no alternatives; obey the mandatory boundaries or go to jail.

We have examined legal and mandatory boundaries. Now we need to take a look at personal boundaries we set for ourselves. Obviously the Ten Commandments were given as a rule and guide for our faith.

The Personal Boundaries should be a rule and guide for our actions. Perhaps the Ten Commandments and the Personal Boundaries are over-lapping and that's O.K.

The Personal Boundaries would include a set of Thou Shall Not personal dynamics, i.e.

1. **MORAL**: Thou Shall Not do anything that would compromise your belief system or be contrary to the doctrines of your church, or compromise your conscienous.
2. **ETHICAL**: Thou Shall Not cheat on your Income Tax Statement, file fraudulent insurance claim forms, refuse to give back too much money you have been given in change, etc.
3. **HONESTY**: Thou Shall Not Lie; you have heard it said *"a little white lie is O.K."* This statement is a fallacy; a white lie is not the truth. It may be half- truth but it is, nevertheless, a whole lie. A lie is a lie, is a lie!
4. **INTEGRITY**: Integrity attests to character. When you tell someone you will do something and you don't do it you have not only lied, you have compromised your integrity. A person is only as good as their word.

The moral boundaries direct, reinforce and support an individual's moral compass.

To summarize, the only way to claim victory in adhering to boundaries, is simply to recognize the boundaries, obey the law, keep a positive attitude, and facilitate ***the applied power of positive thinking,***

Vignette:

Brian hated school. He got teased and bullied about his long neck, skinny body and acne. All of those he once called "friends" at one time had seemingly abandoned him; except one, Keith who he considered to be his "best" friend. Keith had befriended him. Keith, too, felt like a misfit. Keith was a slow learner and mildly mentally challenged. He had been placed in exceptional student classes. But his parents objected. They wanted him to remain in the student general population instead of a special education program.

Because of his handicap Keith had become the butt of jokes by his peers. The rejection and differences had drawn them together; they quickly bonded in friendship. Brian's rejection by peers precipitated in deviant behavior. He had refused to do homework assignments and his grades had fallen.

Both of Keith's parents worked. Keith had been a latch-key kid since age 10. The parents over compensated their love for him by giving him just about anything he wanted. They each felt guilty for having to work to make ends meet, and leave him alone and unsupervised in the home.

Their guilt was exacerbated to the point where they felt they were neglecting his childhood. They showered him with gifts and overcompensation; then they divorced.

Brian would often go to Keith's home; he learned that the parents were actually the grandparents who were raising him in the absence of his mother who was in a correctional facility for drug abuse and possession; his father had abandoned the family and divorced his mother.

Brian appeared to be a good kid and was liked by Keith's grandparents, Mr. and Mrs. who Ronald Kelly, who believed he would have a strong influence on Keith. Therefore, Brian was readily accepted into the home of Keith's grandparents; they had no idea that he would violate their trust.

As the grandparents had hoped for Keith was strongly influenced by Brian and they continued to pal around and be buddies. Too late, the grandparents learned the influence Brian had on Keith would be negative.

When Brian and Keith were alone in the grandparents home Brian would often admire the gun collection Keith's grandfather had locked away in a gun closet. In their den they also had a wet bar where multiple kinds of liquor were kept for his grandfather's guest entertainment.

As their friendship bonded Brian encouraged Keith to start sampling the different kinds of liquor. The violation of trust continued and they began to sample more and more of the alcohol to the point of getting a buzz on. In one instance in a semi-drunken state Brian convinced Keith to unlock his grandfather's gun cabinet so they could handle the guns; although none of the guns were loaded the grandfather did have boxes of ammo in the drawer of the gun cabinet.

Over his friend Keith's objection, Brian would take the guns out of the case and play with them. On one occasion Keith's grandfather discovered the gun cabinet unlocked and asked Keith about it. Keith lied and denied knowing anything about it.

On another occasion Brian and Keith drank too much and became drunk. Brian fell asleep and when he awakened he discovered Keith had passed out and couldn't be aroused. Frightened he quickly left the home hoping Keith would be awake and sobered up by the time his grandparents come home.

Keith did wake up but still was drunk and threw up on the sofa and all over the living room carpet. Although sympathetic for his alcohol sick grandson, Mr. Kelly was furious. He demanded to know why his usually shy and obedient grandson had betrayed his trust and had opened abused the alcohol and had gotten drunk.

After many refusals to tell "why" he got drunk, in an attempt to protect his friend Brian, Keith finally gave in to his grandfather's relentless questioning. He told his grandfather about Brian. He also confessed to unlocking the gun cabinet so Brian could handle the guns.

His grandfather helped him shower and put him to bed. Keith had also told his grandfather that he and Brian had been cutting classes and ditching school. Keith finally gave in to his grandfather's relentless questioning. He told his grandfather about Brian. He also confessed to unlocking the gun cabinet so Brian could handle the guns.

Keith also told him he and Brian had been cutting classes and ditching school. The next day, with his grandson in tow Mr. Kelly kept an appointment with the school principal. The principal listened attentively to the grandfather's report and then called the school police officer to report the incident, i.e. truancy and betrayal of trust with Keith's grandfather. The police officer immediately notified Brian's parents who grounded Brain for three months with no extracurricular activities.

The Kelly's also grounded Keith and withdrew him from the general school population and returned him to the special education class program. They also forbid Keith to have any further contact with Brian.

Keith thrived in the special education program and in the new more sensitive environment and became a high-achiever beyond the Kelly grandparent's expectations.

The same could not be said for Brian. He consistently violated his parents grounding restriction and received stronger discipline at both home and school.

A month before the school year ended Brian went missing. Late in the day he was discovered in his parent's garage hanging from a rope attached to a rafter; he had hanged himself in a teen-suicide.

Keith's grandparents had acted responsibly in taking immediate steps to correct a potentially dangerous situation involving their grandson Keith, which could have also ended in tragedy.

This is an excellent and explicit illustration of how appropriate value-judgment can be responsible for successful achievement.

At the end of the day; *success*: By applying boundaries, and value-judgment, combined with facilitation of ***the applied power of positive thinking.***

CHAPTER 30

Closure

Anytime a person has a loss in their life such as the loss of a loved one, a job, a home, or long lived pet, there is an appropriate feeling of overwhelming bereavement, grief and sadness.

Subsequently, there is a need for expression of grief over the loss. People grieve in different way with many different feelings. There is no time frame for bereavement, grief, and sadness. For some, weeks or months are adequate; for others it may take years to grieve the loss.

In an attempt to aid and assist those who may be experiencing loss in their lives the following alternatives are offered for closure.

THE DEATH OF A LOVED ONE:

Usually after the normal grieving stage with tears, bereavement, grief and sadness an individual can work through the bereavement process. However, for others some become stuck at a certain point in the grief process. They just can't seem to get the loss out of their mind.

Therapists, including the author, often suggest different methods for the bereaved person to use which will make their grieving process just a little less difficult.

One of those suggested methods to use is the writing of a letter to the lost loved one.

In the letter they can detail and enumerate what they consider to be important left open issues, unfinished business, and unresolved issues with regard to their relationship to the loved one who has gone on before them.

An example letter form is presented as a guide for the bereaved one to use in expressing their feelings. Obviously, they will want to use their own words in expressing their thoughts and feelings which may help them to experience increased closure in their grief process.

The writing of a letter is simply an alternative method a bereaved person can use to assist them in experiencing increased closure.

THE LETTER:

The letter could begin as follows:

Dear Mother:

Permit me to say that I am your son and I love you; you are my mother. That will never change. Though death can separate us, it can never remove our familial relationship and the cherish memories we have shared. I know I never told you often enough of how much I love you; I do love you and I will never stop loving you. I miss you so much and I think of you all of the time. I go to the phone and catch myself dialing your number like I have done so many times before. In the act of dialing your number I suddenly remember you are no longer alive and I slam down the receiver and break into uncontrollable tears.

My grief turns from bereavement to anger when I remember you died from cirrhosis of the liver from all of the alcohol you drank. I become mad; mad as heck. Because if you had not of been an alcoholic, and drank all of that alcohol, you would still be here. You were too young to die at 62 years of age. You would still be here to enjoy the children and grand children.

Why? Why did you let alcohol take your life? As much as I love you I don't think I will ever be able to forgive you for robbing us of your presence and choosing alcohol over the love of your children. Some times in my darkest moments I hate you for going off and leaving us. But in love or hate, you are never far from my mind; I can't forget you. I love you, but I hate you.

I never took the time to tell you all of these things when you were alive. I didn't want to hurt you. But I need to say them now. I can't hold them inside any longer; I need to express them. And mother, I need to say a final good-bye; I have to release you and let you go.

I close this letter even as I began: You are my mother, I am your son. That will never change. Even in death you are my beloved mother; I love you.

Until we meet again in spirit in that place not made with hands, eternal in the heavens known as Paradise.

Your loving son,
Frank

Please know this is simply an example letter.

What you do with the letter determines how effective it will be in helping to alleviate grief and affect closure. Some suggestions as to what can be done with the letter are:

Take to the cemetery and burn it over the grave or burn it at the niche-side. As the letter is burned and turns to blackened paper and gray ash the bereaved one can commit all of the love, forgiveness, hate, anger or remorse over the loss of the loved one and can be directly communicated to the ash as it spills over the grave or falls at the niche-side. Forever committed and never to be taken back by the grieved one.

The bereaved one will experience a great sense of relief as though a ton of weight has been lifted from their shoulders and their mind will be emptied in part __ but in time __ emptied in full.

The letter can also be mailed to the deceased though standard postal procedures. The effect of receiving the letter at the address of the deceased and opening it has a profound impact in dealing with grief. Upon the bereaved person's receipt and opening of the letter (addressed to the deceased) the bereaved one can take the letter to the bathroom, hold it over the commode, strike a match to it and watch it burn. As the blackened paper turns to gray ash the bereaved one can commit all feelings both positive and negative toward the deceased to the gray ash. After all of the ashes have fallen into the commode the bereaved can simply reach out and flush all of the ash away.

This technique has a powerful impact for the bereaved in helping to cope with the bereavement, grief, and sadness. As with the burning of the letter, over the grave site, or at the niche-side, the bereaved will experience a great sense of relief as though a ton of weight has lifted from their shoulders.

While the letter technique can be effectively used in coping with the loss of a loved one it can also be used for closure for any other occasion of loss.

These are only a few examples of techniques which have proved to be of value in helping bereaved person to cope with their loss and, at the same time, provide a sense of closure in accepting the loss.

Another technique which has proved to be effective is called the empty-chair technique.

THE EMPTY-CHAIR TECHNIQUE:

The bereaved one takes a family photo of the loved one who has passed. Preferably an 8 X 10 inch size; set the photo in an empty chair located in a den, spare bedroom, or other secluded area where there will not be any disturbance by telephone, doorbell, family member entry, etc. The bereaved one will then begin to communicate with the picture of the deceased.

The conversation would be similar to the one-sided-letter discussion specifically tailored to the type of loss, whether death oriented, divorce oriented, long-term employment loss, loss of a valued family pet, etc.

This technique offers opportunity for verbal venting to the photo, (as though the bereaved person was speaking to the deceased in person), at which time words can be expressed to the deceased in anger, in sorrow, in depression, with feelings of blame, or feelings of personal guilt.

Some well-meaning people will attempt to be helpful by asking a grieving friend or relative *"haven't you gotten over your grief yet? It has already been six months."*

Forgive them for their ignorance in not asking, *"How are you dealing with your grief?"* or *"Would you like to talk about your loss?"*

These folks do not intentionally mean to be insensitive. They simply don't know what to say after saying, *"My sincere condolences for your loss."* They are simply at a loss for words.

Speaking of talking about the loss, this is another excellent way for the bereaved to cope with their feelings of grief and work toward closure. The more the bereaved talks about their loss the more accepting they become of the loss.

It needs to be restated that regardless of the technique used by the bereaved there is no one-size-fits-all method or technique. Each person grieves differently. As previously stated, there is no specific time frame for bereavement, grief and sadness.

Each person must grieve at their own pace; for some it will take only weeks, for others it may take months, and still for others it may take years to grieve, accept their loss, and finally experience closure.

Since each person grieves differently, there is no specific time frame for bereavement, grief and sadness, it would be inappropriate to offer a Vignette to illustrate grief and closure.

Suffice it to say that, loss is a part of life; almost without exception everyone has, or will, experience some type of loss.

The important dynamic to remember and focus on is:

The positive aspect gained by being a part of someone's life that has deceased; being part of a divorce from a long-term marital relationship; to have been employed for a certain time at a specific position which ended; to have been good friends with someone who has rejected the friendship; or to have lost a favorite animal pet considered to be a part of the family. One can feel blessed for having been part of that experience and having benefited from it.

Someone has said: *"All good things come to an end,"* believed to be an English Proverb.

Whether this cliché is true for everyone or, in fact, is accepted by anyone, is a matter of choice; it is either accepted or rejected.

The truth of the matter is, regardless of whatever losses we encounter in life, everyone can benefit, cope, and experience closure by adopting and maintaining a positive mental attitude, and by facilitating ***the applied power of positive thinking.***

ENCOURAGEMENT

THINK ABOUT THIS

The person who risks nothing, does nothing, has nothing, Is nothing.

Only a person who risks is free.

William Arthur Ward

TIPS FOR STRESS REDUCTION TECHNIQUES

Eat a balanced diet; three elements are necessary to obtain, and maintain a healthy life. They are: a proper balanced diet; proper rest (7 to 8 Hours per Night), and exercise a minimum of three times per week.

STOP Smoking; REDUCE coffee, tea, caffeine, and carbonated drinks.

Drink 6 to 8 glasses of water per day: At Breakfast; Mid-morning, and Evening

Learn how to say "NO!"

Net-work with others whom you trust.

Develop a Hobby; do something you like outside of work.

Take time for refreshment and entertainment, i.e. read a book; watch TV programs that uplift your spirit; network with other by telephone, texting, or Email.

Provide for you a quiet time for relaxation, reflection and meditation.

Learn to laugh; don't take yourself too seriously.

Recognize your boundaries; use the Serenity Prayer as a Guide:

"God grant me the serenity to accept the things I
cannot change, the courage to change the things I
can, and the wisdom to know the difference."

Make a conscious effort to visualize yourself
as the person you want to be.

Be thankful to God, and others.

Claim your short-comings; take steps to change what you can,
use failures as stepping stones to successful achievement.

Go for a walk; still one of the "best" exercises.

Know your priorities; set goals for achievement:
short term goal; a mid-range goal, and a long-
term goal; diligently work toward obtaining.

Express or "vent" your anger and frustration with someone
you trust; redirect your anger or frustration through exercise.

Develop a routine for regularity in your life; Set times for

Meditation; Meals; Recreation, and Spiritual practices.

Become an "Active Listener;" listen quietly
for people to finish their sentences.

Arrange to have variety in your life with
people, places, thoughts and things.

Frequently "reach outside the box;" stay in touch
with acquaintances, friends, and family.

Laugh often; give yourself permission to laugh at yourself.

Affirm yourself and others, whom you come into contact with.

Make a doable and realistic schedule of tasks you want to
accomplish each day; do not overload the schedule.

When ambulating, walk, don't run or
hurry; hurrying increases stress.

When driving, drive safely, don't speed; STOP when an
amber caution light flashes, don't speed through.

Don't talk on a cell phone while driving.

Don't "Text" and drive.

Take a short "Get Away" vacation. Frequent
"short" vacations are better than long ones.

Think "Good Thoughts" about people you meet.

Always allow time for the "unexpected," to happen.

Always follow the "Golden Rule," that is, "Do unto others, as you would have others do unto you." Matthew 7:12 (Paraphrase).

DEFINITION OF AN AFFIRMATION

Webster's Dictionary defines an affirmation as:

"To confirm; to assert positively; to declare or claim to be true; to ratify."

For the purpose of this writing a more appropriate definition for affirmation would be to reinforce a truth in an individual's life.

In therapy the therapist often encourages a counselee to select an affirmation and use that particular affirmation or affirmations (more than one) to reinforce a weak area in their life.

For example: If an individual has low self-worth and low-self-esteem the therapist might encourage the counselee to select a positive affirmation concerning their weakness, such as,

"I am a confident person."

The therapist would then suggest that the counselee use "removable self-stick notes" to write out the affirmation and place them in multiple places where the counselee would be during the day.

For instance:

1. On the bathroom mirror
2. On the refrigerator
3. On the Front Door
4. On the Automobile rear-view mirror
5. On the computer at home
6. On the bedroom mirror, etc.

The idea is, to have the counselee to repetitiously repeat the affirmation each and every time they come into contact with the note which attests to the positive thought point.

The one-way communication by the counselee to the counselee would be:

"I am O.K.

"Every day I am gaining confidence."

"Every day, in every way, I am getting stronger and stronger."

This is the basic premise for elevating the counselee's mood, increasing confidence, and increasing self-esteem and self-worth.

AN AFFIRMATION PRAYER OF ST. FRANCIS OF ASSISI

Lord, make me an instrument of Thy Peace

Where there is hatred, let me show love.

Where there is injury, pardon.

Where there is doubt, faith.

Where there is despair, hope.

Where there is darkness, light.

Where there is sadness, joy.

O Divine Master,

Grant that I may not so much seek

To be consoled as to console;

To be understood as to understand,

To be loved as to love;

For it is in giving that we receive,

It is in pardoning that we are pardoned,

And it is in dying that we are born to

Eternal life.

AN AFFIRMATION

Every day,

In Every Way,

I Am

Getting

Better

And

Stronger.

AN AFFIRMATION

I

Want

To Be

The Best

Person

I Know

How

To Be.

AN AFFIRMATION

I

Like

Me.

AN AFFIRMATION

I'm

O.K.

AN AFFIRMATION

I

Will

Change

When

I

Need

To.

AN AFFIRMATION

People

Like

Me For

What

I Am.

AN AFFIRMATION

I

Am

A

Faithful

Friend

To

Others.

AN AFFIRMATION

I

Am

A

Good

Person.

AN AFFIRMATION

I

Am

A

Confident

Person.

AN AFFIRMATION

It's

Good

To

Be

Alive.

AN AFFIRMATION

Life

Can

Always

Get

Better.

AN AFFIRMATION

I

Take

Charge

And

Stay

In

Control

Of

My

Life.

AN AFFIRMATION

I

Forgive

Those

Who

Have

Offended

Me.

AN AFFIRMATION

I

Always

Have

Positive

Thoughts.

AN AFFIRMATION

I

Am

Accepted

By

Others.

AN AFFIRMATION

I

Forgive

Myself

For

What

I Have

Done,

And

What

I

Have

Failed

To

Do.

AN AFFIRMATION

I

Am

Successful.

AN AFFIRMATION

I

Am

An

Over-

Achiever.

AN AFFIRMATION

I

Am

In

Control

Of

Time

Management.

Note: Information appearing (in part) on *Encouragement, Tips for Stress Relief,* and *Affirmations* was first published May 2013 under Copyright by author Dr. Curtis E. Smith in his Fourth Book titled *"Walking Through The Valley."* It is used here with permission of the Copyright holder Dr. Curtis E. Smith.

ABOUT THE AUTHOR

The Rev. Dr. Curtis E. Smith is an ordained, non-denominational Minister.

He holds graduate degrees in, marriage and family counseling, religious education, and human behavior. He holds post-graduate degrees in psychology, religion and human behavior.

"Dr. Curtis," as he is fondly called by associates, and colleagues, has extensive education and experience working in private practice as a Counselor, Pastoral Psychotherapist, Marriage / Family Counselor; in the Medical Field as a Counselor and Spiritual Care Coordinator, in both acute hospital care and hospice care program settings.

He is a published author and has written five books on family, hospice care, and religion dealing with life, spirituality and infinity. He has a Clinical Pastoral educational background having trained with a credentialed Clinical Pastoral Education Training Center operated by the Crystal Cathedral located in the state of California.

For many years, Dr. Curtis Smith was in private practice working As a clinical pastoral psychotherapist. He currently works as a Counselor / Spiritual Care Coordinator in the Hospice Industry.

He resides with his family in Anaheim, California.